CONTENTS

GOAL KING #1

MAGIC MESSI

THE GREATEST PLAYER ON THE PLANET

FCB

10 MESSI FACTS

He was just 13 when he left Argentina to join Barcelona's Under-14 side.

Messi's journey from the youth ranks to the first-team came in a record space of time, making his debut in a friendly against Porto aged just 16.

His full Barcelona debut was in 2004 when he helped Barcelona lift the title.

Messi became the youngest player to score a league goal for Barca, at the age of 17 years, ten months and seven days.

He insists that he would NEVER sign for Real Madrid, Barcelona's biggest rivals.

The Argentina forward can play wide, in the middle or as an out and out striker. He is dangerous wherever he plays!

Modest Messi was in awe after being handed the No.10 shirt at Barca, worn previously by his hero Ronaldinho.

He started his own foundation, funded by some of the cash he earns from promotion and sponsorship work. It helps the education and health of underprivileged children.

Messi says he will only be a legend if he helps Argentina win the World Cup.

Messi has been wearing the F50 adiZero micoach boot from adidas – the ones that tell you how far you have run. Bet Messi's distance was a very long way!

He's a football genius. The player whose footballing skills you can't help but admire.

And having won the past three World Player of the Year awards there can be no disputing the fact that Lionel Messi is quite simply the greatest player around at the moment.

The Barcelona and Argentina star isn't the tallest but he is a giant once he pulls on his famous boots.

He's so good that he doesn't even have to think what he is doing with a football, Messi's magic feet do all the talking necessary on a football pitch.

And sometimes even his teammates can only stand and watch in awe as he slaloms past opposition defenders to slot the ball past struggling keepers.

Many of his fellow professionals admit they would pay hard cash to watch Messi in action and that some of his ball skills leave them perched on the edge of their seats.

Messi admits: "To me, football is the most important thing. It is more important than the money and the personal glory

"When I am running with the ball, nothing else matters and I think I am the only person that exists in the entire planet. When I am playing football I am totally free, no amount of awards or money can buy you freedom that is why I am so totally in love with the game."

WHAT THEY THINK ABOUT HIM...

"He is the best in the world, simple as that. He is a player that when any kid watches him, wants to be him. He is not just a player – technically he is the best in the world – he works hard for the team and that's what makes him the person and the player that he is. You watch him and it's like watching an eight or nine-year-old play."

DAVID BECKHAM, LA Galaxy, former England captain

"Luckily we have the best player in the world. Messi is everything for the Seleccion, we will not find anyone better. He is a very important player to the group and they listen to him in all of the meetings."

SERGIO BATISTA, Argentina coach

"Messi is brilliant. No one in the world has the talent that Messi has."

FABIO CAPELLO, Former England boss

"Messi is a great player and rightly World Player of the Year. For every footballer out there, not just me, that's the target you want to try to get to and, hopefully, I can."

WAYNE ROONEY, Manchester United and England striker

MESSI'S RECORD

73 GOALS IN SEASON 2011-12!

GOALS GALORE!

LA LIGA:	50
UEFA SUPER CUP:	1
SPANISH CUP:	3
SPANISH SUPER CUP:	3
CHAMPIONS LEAGUE:	14
CLUB WORLD CUP:	2

GOAL KING #2
ROCKIN' RONNIE!

Cristiano Ronaldo scored a staggering 60 goals in season 2011-12 for Real Madrid.

And Sir Alex Ferguson, the Manchester United manager who sold him for a world record £80m, reckons the midfielder is now worth TEN TIMES the amount he was sold for in 2009.

Premier League fans mostly remember Ronaldo for his step-overs but since move to the Bernabeu he has also become an even more lethal finisher than he was at Old Trafford.

Of course he did MISS a penalty for Madrid in the Champions League semi-final against Bayern Munich, which just shows that he is human!

Many clubs would love to buy the Portugal star but he insists: "I'm very happy at the club.

"I've just had my third season with Real Madrid and I always try to do my best when I put this jersey on. Things have been going the way I want and hopefully, it will remain being like that for a long time."

Despite his flash cars and celebrity lifestyle Ronaldo admits that he is superstitious in his pre-match routines.

"Regardless of who we face, I do everything the same way. The adrenaline might be slightly higher for certain games, simply because of the difficulty level of the game itself, but I always think about winning, no matter who the opponent is," he said.

Ronaldo's sometimes been accused of being big-headed or believing that he's the top man in the team. But reality is a bit different…

"I have to thank my team-mates, because without them, I certainly wouldn't be able to score these goals. I'm not seeking personal records, but rather trophies for the club," he added.

WHAT THEY THINK ABOUT HIM...

"His stats are simply incredible and the truth is, I never expected he could get so far and so soon, by assuming such an important role in the team. He has already surpassed other big names."

IKER CASILLAS,
Real Madrid captain

"If both Messi and Cristiano Ronaldo were born in different eras, they would have ruled the football scene and collected 10 FIFA Balon d'Ors each."

JOSE MOURINHO,
Real Madrid manager

"That was a fantastic buy for them at £80m. We thought that's not bad. Now we are saying it should've been £300 million!"

SIR ALEX FERGUSON,
Man United manager

RONNIE'S RECORD

MAN UNITED
292 games
118 goals

REAL MADRID
144 games
146 goals
(to 2011-12)

GOALS 2011-12

LA LIGA:	46
SPANISH CUP:	3
COPA DEL REY:	1
CHAMPIONS LEAGUE:	10
TOTAL:	60

CHAMPIONS OF EUROPE

It might not have been Chelsea's first choice side with captain John Terry suspended, but the boys in Blue who captured the club's first-ever European Cup certainly turned out to be a dream team for fans.

They were also a dream side for Roberto de Matteo who, even as interim manager, managed to win the Champions League title, something so many of his big-name predecessors had failed to do. With the game still locked at 1-1 after extra-time it went to a dramatic penalty shoot-out… and the Blues held their nerve.

THE PENALTY SHOOT-OUT

Philipp Lahm scores - Bayern 1 Chelsea 0
Mata shot saved - Bayern 1 Chelsea 0
Mario Gomez scores - Bayern 2 Chelsea 0
David Luiz fires home - Bayern 2 Chelsea 1
Keeper Neur notches - Bayern 3 Chelsea 1
Lampard pulls one back - Bayern 3 Chelsea 2
Olic shot saved - Bayern 3 Chelsea 2
Cole equalises - Bayern 3 Chelsea 3
Bastian Schweinsteiger fails - Bayern 3 Chelsea 3
Cool Drogba his the winner! Bayern 3 Chelsea 4

MISSING FROM ACTION

JOHN TERRY
Suspended for the final after a red card in the semis. The captain would have been first on the team sheet if available for selection.

BRATISLAV IVANOVIC
The Serbia defender would also have been in for the final if not suspended. He picked up a yellow card in the semi-final, unaware he was walking a disciplinary tightrope.

RAMIRES
The Brazil midfielder was also a semi-final yellow card recipient, which ruled him out of the final.

RAUL MEIRELES
Like Ramires and Ivanovic, battling Portugal midfielder Meireles failed in a bid to have his suspension lifted after a semi-final yellow card.

EXTRA TIME This was Chelsea's first European Cup win. Real Madrid have won the trophy nine times, AC Milan seven, five for Liverpool; Bayern Munich, Barcelona and Ajax all four times. Man United are three-times winners with Inter Milan.

THE TEAM THAT PLAYED

PETR CECH
One of the best keepers in the Premier League, the Czech Republic star hit top form in games leading up to the final and maintained that during the Bayern clash with some great stops. Saved Arjen Robben's penalty.

JOSE BOSINGWA
Chelsea fans expected him to give them a few nightmares and it was close on a couple of occasions as he got tested to the limit by Bayern's tricky winger Franck Ribery. Did better than many supporters feared he might.

GARY CAHILL
Came back from injury to plug the gaps at the back and performed admirably. Wasn't expected to last the distance – but he did, and came through with flying colours.

DAVID LUIZ
Another who returned after injury because of Chelsea's limited options. The Brazil defender had a few shaky moments but for most of the final he played his part. We're not sure about that hair!

ASHLEY COLE
Superb! The England left back rarely has a poor game but in this final he was outstanding. Often the difference between Bayern and the Blues.

JOHN OBI MIKEL
Never the most popular of players among Stamford Bridge fans but he certainly won them over at the Allianz Arena. Had to work hard to earn his medal.

FRANK LAMPARD
After a slow start Chelsea's midfield marvel grew into the game and just edged his battle with the Germans in the centre of the park. The stand-in captain has rightly earned his place in Blues' history.

SALOMON KALOU
Had to play in a more withdrawn role to battle the Germans' power in midfield but stuck to his task. Would have much preferred to operate as a forward.

JUAN MATA
Missed his spot-kick in the penalty shoot-out and didn't produce the kind of top form he had all season. But an FA Cup and Champions League winners' medals in your first season can't be bad. A great end to a superb debut season for the club.

RYAN BERTRAND
His European debut – and what a first game! Played like a veteran, defended, attacked and showed he has no fear despite the pedigree of some of the players he faced.

DIDIER DROGBA
The legend got bigger! Scored a brilliant equaliser and then showed nerves of solid steel to slot home his penalty shoot-out spot-kick to seal the Blues' victory. His place in football history is now assured.

SUBS
FLORENT MALOUDA
Came on for Bertrand despite carrying a niggling injury himself.

FERNANDO TORRES
Showed a few promising touches when he came on for Kalou. Surprisingly wasn't allowed to take one of the deciding penalties.

UNUSED SUBS
Ross Turnbull, keeper. Michael Essien, midfielder. Oriol Romeu, midfielder. Paulo Ferreira, defender. Daniel Sturridge, striker.

THE BAYERN MUNICH SIDE
Neuer, Lahm, Boateng, Tymoschuk, Contento, Schweinsteiger, Kroos, Robben, Mueller (van Buyten), Ribery (Olic), Gomez. Subs not used: Butt, Petersen, Rafinha, Usami, Pranjic.

EXTRA TIME UEFA, who run the Champions League and are European football's governing body, agreed to a Chelsea request that banned captain John Terry should be allowed to lift the trophy despite having to sit out the final in Munich.

FAMOUS FACES

CAN YOU RECOGNISE THESE TOP FOOTBALL PERSONALITIES FROM THEIR PICTURES FROM THE PAST? WE'VE GIVEN YOU THE YEAR IN WHICH THEY WERE TAKEN AND A FEW CLUES. YOU WILL BE AMAZED AT WHO SOME OF THEM ARE...

1985

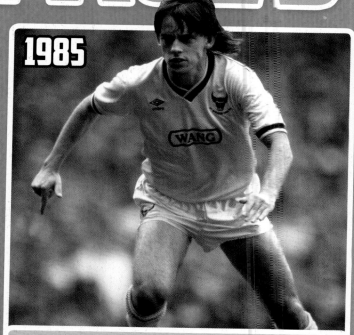

This one's going to catch you out! Believe us when we say that the years have seen a few changes. We will tell you he used to play for Arsenal and that he had managerial success last season.

1982

Two Scots, one a player the other his boss. Now both have been or are top managers in England. Bonus if you get them both right (one's on this page in his own right).

1987

Hat a boy! This guy's now officially a pensioner – but we bet you wouldn't tell him to stop managing or stop adding to the mountain of trophies he's won!

1989

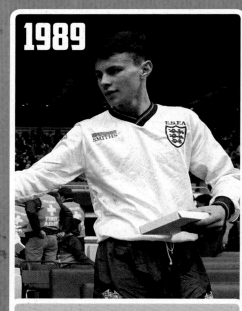

Now this one could catch you out! All we will say is that you should take no notice of that shirt as a clue to his future international appearances, although this Premier League megastar DID actually wear it during this game.

1990

He was more of a striker of the ball rather than a juggler! This one-time record-breaking hitman is now a television pundit.

EXTRA TIME Sir Alex Ferguson was boss of Aberdeen where he won three Scottish title before taking over as manager of Manchester United in 1986. Up to the end of season 2011-12 he had won 12 Premier League titles

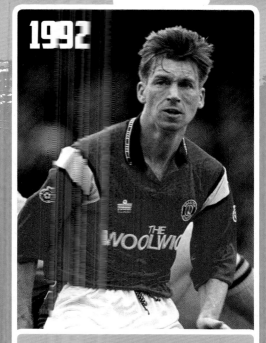

1992

Division One, no prizes that he was playing for Charlton – who he later managed – but do you recognise this Premier League boss who can normally be spotted in a suit?

2000

An easy one for you! Just over a decade ago yet he was still Kopping goals for his team…

YOUR ANSWERS

1982

1985

1987

1989

1990

1992

2000

THE DIFFICULT GAME!

HOW MUCH DO YOU KNOW ABOUT OUR FAVOURITE GAME? HERE'S YOUR CHANCE TO FINE OUT IN OUR AMAZING FOUR-PART QUIZ!

1. Who has played for the most clubs, Joey Barton or Dimitar Berbatov

A: ....

2. Michael Essien and Patrice Evra have both played for Lyon. True or false?

A: ....

3. Bastian Schweinsteiger has played for just one club. Which one?

A: ....

4. Name Ireland keeper Shay Given's first club in England.

A: ....

5. What nationality is striker Alexis Sanchez?

A: ....

6. What position does Bacary Sagna play?

A: ....

7. From which Dutch club did Newcastle buy Cheick Tiote?

A: ....
....

8. For which international side does Eden Hazard play?

A: ....

9. The Toure brothers, Yaya and Kolo, play for which international side?

A: ....

10. Which League One club borrowed Arsenal keeper Wojciech Szczesny?

A: ....

11. What nationality is Tottenham's Rafael van der Vaart?

A: ....

12. Born in Yugoslavia, this Manchester United defender plays for Serbia.

A: ....

COPY

13. Leighton Baines joined Everton from which other Premier League side?

A: ....

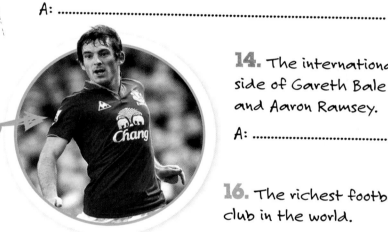

14. The international side of Gareth Bale and Aaron Ramsey.

A: ....

15. Striker Newcastle signed for £10m in January 2012.

A: ....

16. The richest football club in the world.

A: ....

17. The keeper who kept 21 Premier League clean sheets in 2004-05.

A: ....

18. Manager who has won the European Cup as both a player and manager.

A: ....

....

19. Who scored the Premier League's 15,000th goal?

A: ....

20. In which country do mega-rich Anzhi Makhachkala play?

A: ....

ФУТБОЛЬНЫЙ КЛУБ
АНЖИ
МАХАЧКАЛА

1991

SPOT THE BOSS

THERE'S NO ESCAPING THE SHOOT PHOTOGRAPHERS! SIX TOP MANAGERS WENT ON A SECRET SCOUTING MISSION — WATCHING ONE OF THE MOST PROMISING YOUNG PLAYERS IN FOOTBALL. THEY THOUGHT THEY WOULDN'T BE SPOTTED — BUT THEY DIDN'T BANK ON US BEING THERE! CAN YOU FIND THEM LURKING AMONG THE FANS?

EXTRA TIME

Roberto Mancini, who guided Manchester City to the 2011-12 Premier League title, won three Serie A titles as boss of Inter Milan. The former Leicester City midfielder has also be the manager at Fiorentina and Lazio.

HERE ARE THE SIX BOSSES FOR YOU TO FIND:

ROBERTO MANCINI **ALAN PARDEW** **ARSENE WENGER**

IAN HOLLOWAY **HARRY REDKNAPP** **SAM ALLARDYCE**

EXTRA TIME Tottenham manager Harry Redknapp has also been the gaffer at Bournemouth, West Ham United, Portsmouth (twice) and Southampton. He led Pompey to victory in the FA Cup in 2008.

SHOOT ANNUAL 2013 **15**

20 GLORIOUS SEASONS!

THE INCREDIBLE ENDING TO 2011-12 EARNED IT THE VOTE AS THE BEST SEASON OF THE PREMIER LEAGUE'S 20 YEARS. A PANEL OF EXPERTS AND THE PUBLIC BOTH VOTED ON OTHER MEMORABLE MOMENTS SINCE THE COMPETITION BEGAN IN 1992-92. THIS IS WHAT THEY DECIDED...

PREMIER LEAGUE 20 SEASONS

GOAL

The public voted Manchester United and England striker Wayne Rooney's overhead kick against Manchester City at Old Trafford as the No.1 goal. Rooney's spectacular strike in February 2011 beat Dennis Bergkamp's 2002 goal at Newcastle, where he flicked the ball, turned and finished at St. James' Park. His team-mate Thierry Henry was third for his flick and volley at Highbury in 2000 against Manchester United.

MATCH

Fans decided the Best Match was the September 2009 result of Manchester United 4 Manchester City 3, when Michael Owen scored the winner six minutes into stoppage time. Second was Liverpool 4 Newcastle 3 (April 1996) and third Liverpool 4 Arsenal 4 (April 2009).

PLAYER

Ryan Giggs, the only man to have played and scored in all 20 seasons, was a fitting winner. He had already been playing a year before the Premier League kicked off! "Being named as the best player in the 20 Seasons of the Premier League is a tremendous honour for me, and very humbling when you consider some of the brilliant players who were nominated alongside me " said Giggs.

SAVE

Sunderland and Scotland keeper Craig Gordon won Best Save for his stop against Bolton Wanderers in December 2010. He used his left hand at close range to push a shot from Zat Knight over the crossbar.

MANAGER

No surprise that **Sir Alex Ferguson** was handed the top boss award after picking up 12 titles. He is also the only boss to manage in all 20 of the Premier League years. He beat off the challenge of Harry Redknapp, Arsene Wenger, David Moyes and Jose Mourinho.

TEAM

Arsenal's Invincibles, who went the whole of season 2003-04 unbeaten, were voted the Best Team. In total the Gunners went on a 49-game unbeaten run which stretched from May 2003 to October 2004.

GOAL CELEBRATION

King **Eric Cantona** lifted the award for his routine after scoring for Man United against Sunderland in 1996. Cantona had run from the halfway line, played a one-two with Brian McClair and then chipped the ball over keeper Lionel Perez. Cantona then pirouetted on the spot, took in the fans' adulation then held his arms aloft as McClair arrived to celebrate his goal.

QUOTE

Newcastle United manager **Kevin Keegan** won the most memorable quote for his rant on Sky Sports against Manchester United boss Sir Alex Ferguson in 1996. The Geordies were in the race for the title at the time. Keegan said: *"You can tell him now, we're still fighting for this title and he's got to go to Middlesbrough and get something. And I'll tell you, honestly, I will love it if we beat them. Love it."*

FANTASY TEAM

The experts and fans were both asked to pick their fantasy teams… and there were only two differences! The experts made two changes to the side picked by supporters, bringing in Rio Ferdinand for Nemanja Vidic and Roy Keane for Steven Gerrard.

Peter Schmeichel (above right)

Ashley Cole, Tony Adams (above left) Nemanja Vidic, Gary Neville

Ryan Giggs, Paul Scholes, Steven Gerrard (below left), Cristiano Ronaldo

Thierry Henry, Alan Shearer (below right)

DANNY WELBECK
Manchester United and England striker

FACT FILE

DANIEL WELBECK

Position: Striker
Birth date: November 26, 1990
Birth place: Manchester
Height: 1.85m (6ft 1 n)
Clubs: Manchester Un ted, Preston North End (loan), Sunderland (loan)
International: England

WELBECK ON...

ENDING GOAL DROUGHTS

"You can't let these things play on your mind, you just play your normal game and, as long as the team keeps winning, that's the main thing. I don't want to just settle for making it, I want to make it as big as possible."

HIS PROGRESS

"I don't sit there and think it will all fall into place. It's time to work harder and take heed of the manger's words and push on. Hopefully one day I will be an integral part of the set up."

HIS APPROACH

"I go into every game like I am playing at school, looking forward to getting on the pitch and getting the ball. I'm not really the nervous type and I don't get fazed. When I made my England debut [against Ghana, who he could have played for] I even had a few cousins in the stands booing. We all had a little laugh at the end."

SIR ALEX FERGUSON

"The manager shows time and time again he will give local players a chance and it is up to the ind vidual to take it. I've been brought up to play the game and not the occasion. At United they have always drilled that into us, to win and enjoy yourself. I have that mentality not to be overawed by anything."

WELBECK FACTS

1. Welbeck hopes that he and United team mate Wayne Rooney can become the No.1 partnership for club and country.

2. Welbeck also qualified to play for Ghana – even after making his England against them! That first game was a friendly – but when he pulled on the Three Lions shirt for the game against Montenegro that committed him to the England cause.

3. His two big heroes when he was a youngster were Arsenal's France striker Thierry Henry and Ryan Giggs, now his United team mate!

4. He was a sub who was subbed by England Under-21 boss Stuart Pearce but says that he accepted having to come off as he wasn't playing well.

5. Welbeck made his Premier League debut in November 2008 when he was a scoring substitute at Old Trafford in a 5-0 victory over Stoke City.

WHAT HIS BOSS SAYS...

"He's got a great future. He can gallop really quickly, he's a good footballer and he's got a great attitude when he loses the ball."

Sir Alex Ferguson, *United manager*

EXTRA TIME Welbeck, who was nine days short of his 18th birthday when he made his United debut, was checked out by rivals City when he was eight-years-old. They said he wasn't good enough. United spotted him a week later.

PROFILE
SCOTT SINCLAIR
Swansea City winger

FACT FILE

SCOTT ANDREW SINCLAIR

Position: Winger
Birth date: March 25, 1989
Birth place: Bath, Avon
Height: 1.77m (5ft 10in)
Clubs: Bristol Rovers, Chelsea, Plymouth (loan), QPR (loan), Charlton (loan), Crystal Palace (loan), Birmingham City (loan), Wigan (loan), Swansea City
International: England Under-21

SINCLAIR ON...

PRESSURE

"I've proved I can handle pressure, every player likes to play in the big, high pressure games. I think it brings out the best in me. I think adding more pressure to the game helps you as a player."

BEING A SUB

"I get frustrated on the bench as I always like to start. I just have to do my best and make an impact when I play. Sometimes you get picked, sometimes you don't. I can wait for that."

PREMIER LEAGUE

"It is fantastic for the fans, being in the Premier League, I think we surprised a few people. Everyone who comes to our ground will have a little think when they are playing us."

TAKING PENALTIES

"There's no doubt it's getting harder for me to score penalties because goalkeepers are doing their homework and studying videos. That's the challenge for me – to keep them guessing. I won't be shirking my responsibility. If we get another penalty I'll be ready."

WHAT HIS FORMER BOSS SAYS...

"He puts defenders on the back foot. He gets down the sides and in between people, he is a goal scorer. The most important thing is he is a real threat all the time."
Brendan Rodgers, *the manager who brought Sinclair to Swansea City*

5 SINCLAIR FACTS

1 The midfielder cost Chelsea a total of £750,000 after joining them from Bristol Rovers in 2005 but started just one Premier League games in five years.

2. After loans to six different clubs, he moved to Swansea in July 2010 for £1m, which was then a club record buy.

3. Swansea's first-ever goal in the top-flight was a penalty scored by Sinclair against West Bromwich Albion.

4. Although he has played for England at all levels up to Under-21, Jamaica have tried to get him to play for their senior side.

5. Sinclair scored a play-off final hat-trick against Reading to earn Swansea promotion to the Premier League for the first time ever in 2011.

EXTRA TIME Brendan Rodgers, who took Swansea into the Premier League, worked as a coach at Chelsea when Sinclair was on the books at Stamford Bridge. When Sinclair helped the Swans stay up it added an extra £1m to his transfer

MEDALLION MEN

THEY EARN LOADS OF MONEY — BUT ASK ANY PROFESSIONAL FOOTBALLER
WHAT HE WANTS AND THE ANSWER WILL BE: SILVERWARE!
THESE GUYS HAVE AWARDS THEY WILL NEVER FORGET...

JOHN TERRY

Three Premier League titles, five FA Cups, two League Cups and a European Cup so far means the Chelsea captain has a lot to remember from his career as a no-nonsense defender. But it was the first of those Premiership wins, in 2005, that will be forever remembered by the England centre half. Not only did his side have the most clean sheets and most points ever recorded. It was also the first time in 50 years that the Blues had lifted the top-flight title.
BORN: Dec 7, 1980. PLACE: Barking, Essex

GAEL CLICHY

Gael Clichy was just 18 when he won a Premier League medal with Arsenal. He was a member of the Gunners "Invincibles" – the team that went through a whole season unbeaten. He also won the FA Cup in 2005. His superb form saw the France left back take over from England defender Ashley Cole when he moved to Chelsea. Clichy joined Manchester City in summer 2011 and now has another Premier League winner's medal.
BORN: July 26, 1985. PLACE: Toulouse, France

STEVEN GERRARD

Steven Gerrard will forever be remembered for a night in Istanbul in May 2005 when he inspired Liverpool to a famous Champions League victory. It was the fifth time the Reds had lifted Europe's biggest crown but it was more than just a local hero making good. Liverpool trailed 3-0 at half-time to AC Milan and it looked over. Man of the Match Gerrard then scored the first of his side's three goals that took the game to extra-time and a penalty shoot-out which they won. Gerrard also has two FA Cups and three League Cups to his credit.
BORN: May 30, 1980. PLACE: Whiston, Liverpool

RYAN GIGGS

At the end of season 2010-11, Giggs had won a record 12 Premier League titles. It's a total that will take some beating! The Wales winger has been at Old Trafford since he was just 14-years-old, and is a rare one-club player. He's now made more than 900 appearances for United, including 600-plus in the League. Oh, and he's also won four FA Cups, four League Cups, two Champions Leagues, eight Community Shields, a UEFA Super Cup, Intercontinental Cup and FIFA Club World Cup! **BORN: November 29, 1973. PLACE: Cardiff, Wales**

EXTRA TIME Rangers have won more domestic league titles than any other club in the world. Founded in 1872 they won their first title in 1891 and up to the end of 2011-12 they had bagged a total of 54. Celtic have 43 Scottish titles.

ONES TO WATCH

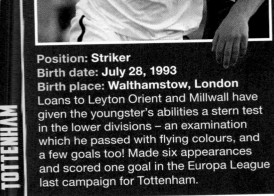

HARRY KANE
TOTTENHAM

Position: Striker
Birth date: July 28, 1993
Birth place: Walthamstow, London
Loans to Leyton Orient and Millwall have given the youngster's abilities a stern test in the lower divisions – an examination which he passed with flying colours, and a few goals too! Made six appearances and scored one goal in the Europa League last campaign for Tottenham.

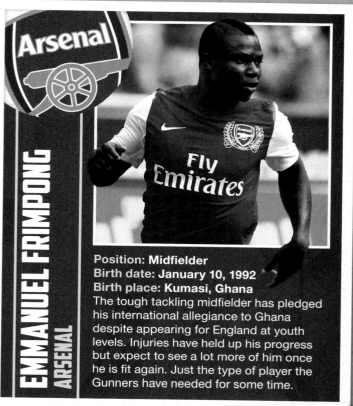

EMMANUEL FRIMPONG
ARSENAL

Position: Midfielder
Birth date: January 10, 1992
Birth place: Kumasi, Ghana
The tough tackling midfielder has pledged his international allegiance to Ghana despite appearing for England at youth levels. Injuries have held up his progress but expect to see a lot more of him once he is fit again. Just the type of player the Gunners have needed for some time.

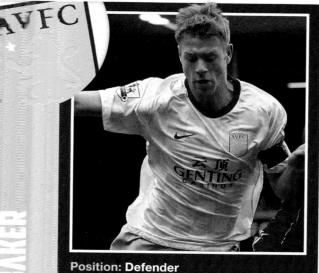

NATHAN BAKER
ASTON VILLA

Position: Defender
Birth date: April 23, 1991
Birth place: Worcester
The England Under-21 player can turn out in central defence or left back. Joined Villa as a 13-year-old and has had loan spells with Lincoln and Millwall. A commanding defender who looks very promising, but needs a bit more experience.

SAMMY AMEOBI
NEWCASTLE UNITED

Position: Striker
Birth date: May 1, 1992
Birth place: Newcastle
Brother of long-serving Newcastle forward Shola, the younger Ameobi has already been eyed up by a number of big clubs despite only a handful of appearances for his home town side. A jack in the box of tricks with a lethal shot.

EXTRA TIME James Milner is the most-capped player for England Under-21s with 46 appearances. Fabrice Muamba and Tom Huddlestone have both appeared 33 times, Michael Mancienne 30, Scott Carson and Steven Taylor both 29.

SHOOT ANNUAL 2013 21

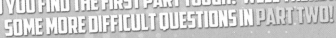

DID YOU FIND THE FIRST PART TOUGH? WELL THERE ARE SOME MORE DIFFICULT QUESTIONS IN PART TWO!

21. How many clubs did Scott Parker play for during the time he won his first four England caps? 1, 2, 3 or 4?

A: ....

23. Name the only team to go through a Premier League season unbeaten.

A: ....

22. What is the name of Barcelona's massive stadium?

A: ....

WOW!

24. The first player to win ten Premier League titles in England (he's now won more!).

A: ....

25. The Amsterdam Arena is home to which Dutch side?

A: ....

26. The two big titles won by Spain in 2008 and 2010.

A: ....

....

27. Manchester United's longest-serving manager.

A: ....

....

28. Denmark midfielder Christian Eriksen was the youngest player at World Cup 2010. How old was he?

A: ....

29. Which famous sportsman did Manchester United winger Ashley Young go to school with?

A: ....

30. What's the name of the ground shared by both Milan sides?

A: ....

31. The number on the back of Lionel Messi's shirt at Barcelona.

A: ....

32. Which Scottish club are known as the Jam Tarts?

A: ....

33. In which country do Flamengo play?

A: ....

34. The first player to score more than 20 Premier League goals for five seasons in a row.

A: ....

....

35. Team that now boasts former England captain David Beckham.

A: ....

36. Welsh team promoted to the Premier League for the first time in 2011

A: ....

37. Crowd capacity of the new Wembley Stadium.

A: ....

38 Name of Arsenal's ground.

A: ....

39. Arsene Wenger has managed two teams in the Champions League. Arsenal and who else?

A: ....

....

WOW!

40. Republic of Ireland's record goalscorer.

A: ....

FAVOURITE PLAYER

TOP FOOTBALLERS NAME THE STARS THAT <u>THEY</u> LOOK UP TO

PAUL SCHOLES
MAN UNITED

"He's a terrific player. When you see him in training and the things he does it's just a joke. I played in his testimonial and thought he was unbelievable."

NOMINATED BY: Phil Jones, Man United and England

CARLOS TEVEZ
ARGENTINA

"He is probably the best player I have played with. Some of the goals he scores and some of the stuff he does in training is just unbelievable."

NOMINATED BY: Adam Johnson, Manchester City and England

LIONEL MESSI
BARCELONA

"Leo is an amazing player and without any doubt the best in the world. I don't want to compare him to legends from the past, I don't think he needs to be compared to others because he is Messi and a brilliant player."

NOMINATED BY: Cesc Fabregas, Spain and Barcelona

EXTRA TIME Lionel Messi, three times World Player of the Year, has a clause in his contract allowing him to leave Barcelona if another team offers £225m! Real Madrid has put a £1 BILLION price tag on the head of Cristiano Ronaldo.

GARETH BALE
TOTTENHAM

"Teams have tried to block him on the flanks but he has started coming into the middle, scoring lots of goals. He is maturing into an outstanding left-winger, probably the best in the Premier League if not in Europe."

NOMINATED BY: Phil Neville, Everton and England

WAYNE ROONEY
MAN UNITED

"It would be a dream to play with Rooney if Manchester United ever came to the point where they needed to sell him. I can't think of one player that plays with the desire of Rooney. You can see the fire in his eyes. It's that fire which makes him the best of the best. He is one of the few talents that can improve this Barcelona team."

NOMINATED BY: Lionel Messi, Barcelona and Argentina

ROBIN VAN PERSIE
HOLLAND

"You just give him anything and he will put it away - left foot, right foot and he has scored a couple of headers as well. He makes it look easy and it's really not. I would love to play up front with him."

NOMINATED BY: Theo Walcott, Arsenal and England

EXTRA TIME — Arsenal bought Holland forward Robin van Persie from Feyenoord in May 2004 for just £2.75m. Gunners boss Arsene Wenger converted him from a winger to striker – the same thing he did with the legendary Thierry Henry!

SHOOT ANNUAL 2013   25

GARY CAHILL
Chelsea and England defender

FACT FILE

GARY JAMES CAHILL

Position: Defender
Birth date: December 19, 1985
Birth place: Sheffield
Height: 1.88 (6ft 2in)
Clubs: Aston Villa, Burnley (loan), Sheffield United (loan), Bolton, Chelsea
International: England

CAHILL ON...

INTERNATIONAL CHANCES

"Staying fit is half of the game if you want to stay up the pecking order. It's a case of biding my time and working hard because sometimes it can be frustrating. All I can do is try and keep playing well and take my chances when they come along. Sometimes I'm in the squad, sometimes I'm not, sometimes I am on the bench, sometimes I am not."

ENGLAND HOPES

"It was fabulous to make my first England appearance alongside John Terry, it made my job a lot easier. Obviously playing with the English boys at Chelsea will help our understanding. But I take nothing for granted. I am came here to work hard and get into the team. I can bring that little bit of English defender, where you just get your head in, get stuck in."

LEAVING BOLTON

"A lot of times nowadays people leave clubs on bad notes but I have got nothing but thanks for Bolton, they gave me the platform and the manager there was fantastic for me. I played for England off the back of playing for Bolton. It is fantastic when you are wanted at a club by the manager and the fans, and it is time for me to try to repay that at Chelsea."

WHAT HIS CAPTAIN SAYS...

"First and foremost, he's a great player. He's a really solid defender. He can play left and right foot, he's great in air and is quick as well."

John Terry, *Chelsea skipper*

5 CAHILL FACTS

1. Cahill signed for the Blues and then gave away the special Chelsea shirt he was handed when he joined the club so that it could be sold to raise cash for The Chelsea Foundation charity.

2. He agreed a five and a half year deal with Chelsea that is believed to be worth £80,000 a week.

3. In his last game for Bolton Cahill scored as his side won at Everton.

4. Cahill was bought by Bolton from Aston Villa for £5m in January 2008 and sold in January 2012 to Chelsea for £7m.

5. The first red card of his career came on December 3, 2011 when Bolton were beaten 3-0 at Tottenham.

EXTRA TIME Gary Cahill signed for Chelsea in mid-January 2012 and by the end of May he had collected an FA Cup medal and helped the Blues to victory in the Champions League! Then he was called up by England for Euro 2012!

FABRICIO COLOCCINI

Newcastle and Argentina defender

FACT FILE

FABRICIO COLOCCINI

Position: Defender
Birth date: January 22, 1982
Birth place: Cordoba, Argentina
Height: 1.85m (6ft 1in)
Clubs: Boca Juniors, AC Milan, San Lorenzo (loan), Alaves (loan), Atletico Madrid (loan), Villarreal (loan), Deportivo, Newcastle
International: Argentina

COLOCCINI ON...

BEING A DEFENDER

"I am calm, I am quite quiet really, but sometimes you need to be like that as a defender. I like to try and anticipate what is going to happen in the game. For the manager to describe me as one of the best defenders he has worked with is also good."

LIONEL MESSI

"On the TV he looks very quick but in life he is quicker. It is unbelievable. When you are live, and it is on the pitch, he is so, so quick. There really is nothing you can do. When I was in training with Argentina, you make sure you're on his team. You want to play with him, not against him."

NEWCASTLE

"Me and my family are happy here in Newcastle. Of course the club has got better since I first came here. We had too many changes but now it is a lot more stable. I hope we can win something for the supporters and for the club. All the players want to do better for the club."

5 COLOCCINI FACTS

1. The defender joined Newcastle from Deportivo in August 2008 for £10.3m.

2. Colo stayed with Newcastle even when they were relegated in 2009 to the Championship and was appointed captain for season 2011-12.

3. Football writers voted him their North East Footballer of the Year in 2011.

4. Coloccini picked up a gold medal at the 2004 Olympics in Athens as part of the Argentina side.

5. Colo signed for Newcastle just weeks after his Argentina team mate Jonas Gutierrez.

WHAT HIS BOSS SAYS...

"He's a top player and so proficient technically. He has done very well and is a really likeable character. He's been brilliant for us. Long may that continue. He will go to any length to play if he can."
Alan Pardew, *Newcastle Manager*

EXTRA TIME A total of 41 Argentine players had appeared in the Premier League up to 2011-12, four of them for Newcastle. Besides Coloccini and Gutierrez, the Magpies had Daniel Cordone (2000-01) and Christian Bassedas (2000-02).

SHOOT ANNUAL 2013 **27**

NAME THE PLAYERS!

FOLLOW THE CLUES AND SEE IF YOU CAN NAME THE PREMIER LEAGUE SILHOUETTE STARS

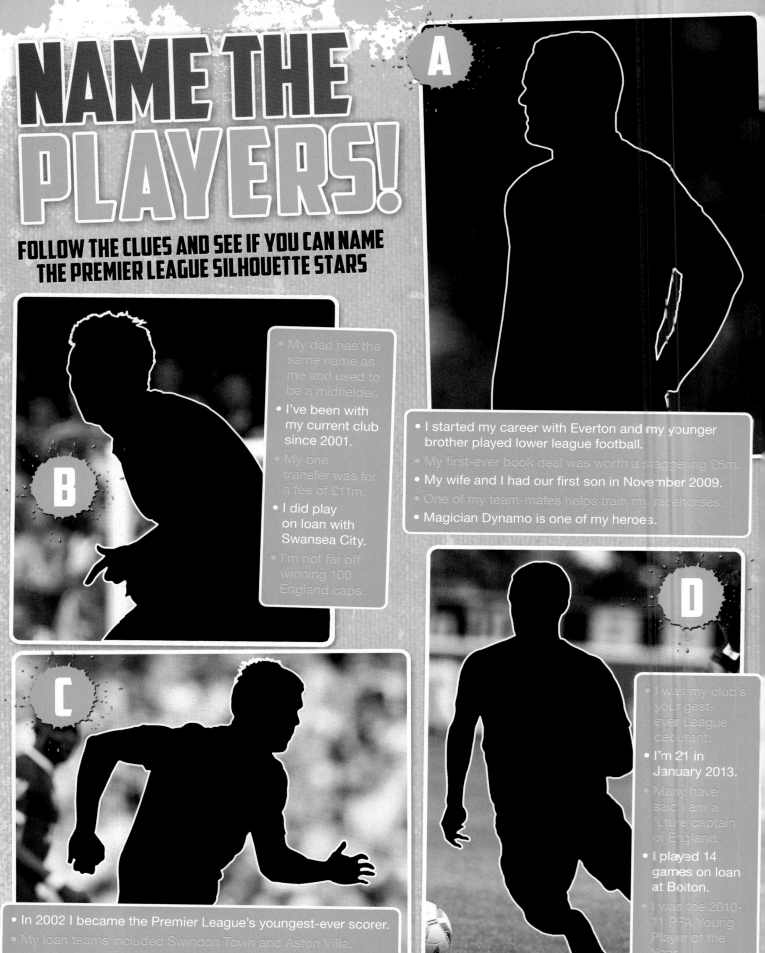

A

- I started my career with Everton and my younger brother played lower league football.
- My first-ever book deal was worth a staggering £5m.
- My wife and I had our first son in November 2009.
- One of my team-mates helps train my racehorses.
- Magician Dynamo is one of my heroes.

B

- My dad has the same name as me and used to be a midfielder.
- I've been with my current club since 2001.
- My one transfer was for a fee of £11m.
- I did play on loan with Swansea City.
- I'm not far off winning 100 England caps.

C

- In 2002 I became the Premier League's youngest-ever scorer.
- My loan teams included Swindon Town and Aston Villa.
- I am the record holder for most England Under-21 caps.
- I can play anywhere in the midfield, full back and even striker.
- After 24 England senior games I had yet to score a goal.

D

- I was my club's youngest-ever League debutant.
- I'm 21 in January 2013.
- Many have said I am a future captain of England.
- I played 14 games on loan at Bolton.
- I was the 2010-11 PFA Young Player of the Year.

EXTRA TIME Former England captain David Beckham went on loan from Manchester United to Preston in 1994-95 before making his Premier League debut. He scored two goals in five games for North End – one direct from a corner!

A

TEAM

NICKNAME

B

TEAM

NICKNAME

C

TEAM

NICKNAME

CHAMPIONSHIP CHALLENGE

THE RACE TO WIN THE CHAMPIONSHIP IS TOUGH — BUT THE REWARDS MASSIVE WITH THREE PREMIER LEAGUE PLACES UP FOR GRABS. TWO TEAMS GO UP AUTOMATICALLY BUT THE THIRD HAS TO WIN THE PLAY-OFF FINAL. WE'VE PRINTED IMAGES OF SIX KITS USED BY TEAMS IN ENGLAND'S SECOND-FLIGHT LAST SEASON. CAN YOU TELL US WHICH TEAMS THEY ARE AND ALSO THE TEAMS' NICKNAMES!

D

TEAM

NICKNAME

E

TEAM

NICKNAME

F

TEAM

NICKNAME

EXTRA TIME — The Championship used to be known as Division Two – when the top-flight was still Division One. When the Premier League was born the second tier became Division One before changing to its present name in 2004.

SHOOT ANNUAL 2013 **29**

SUPER STATS

AMAZING FIGURES FROM THE FANTASTIC WORLD OF FOOTBALL

Petr Cech kept 21 Premier League clean sheets for Chelsea in 2005-06.

Arsenal's Thierry Henry was the first player to score 20 goals or more in five consecutive Premier League seasons.

Referees run an average of eight miles in every game.

Former Newcastle striker Obafemi Martins could cover 100 metres in 10.5 seconds!

Robbie Fowler scored a Premier League hat-trick for Liverpool against Arsenal in 1994-95 in just four minutes.

Reading scored a record 106 Championship points in 2006.

Doncaster lost 34 games in Division Three in 1997-98.

Bournemouth's James Hayter hit a hat-trick in 140 seconds against Wrexham.

Andy Cole was the first player to score five goals in a Premier League game, during Man United's 9-0 win over Ipswich in 1995.

Roy Keane was paid £50,000 a week by Manchester United in 1999-2000, a new record salary.

The 15,000th Premier League goal was scored by Fulham's Moritz Volz in 2006-07.

Bradford City's Jim Fryatt scored after just four seconds against Tranmere in 1964.

Striker Kevin Phillips reached 100 goals in 147 games for Sunderland.

Arsenal scored in 55 consecutive matches between 2002 and 2003.

AFC Wimbledon set a new British record when they went 78 games unbeaten between 2003 and 2004.

Substitute Ole Gunnar scored four for Man United against Forest in 1998-99.

Keeper Paul Robinson scored with an 83-yard free-kick for Tottenham against Watford.

Chelsea's Premier League win in 2005 was their first top-flight title in 50 years.

Midfielder Paul Gascoigne was England's first £2m footballer when he moved from Newcastle to Spurs.

Leeds United, Wolves and Leicester City all had 33 points when they were relegated from the Premier League in 2004.

JORDAN HENDERSON
Liverpool and England midfielder

FACT FILE

JORDAN BRIAN HENDERSON

Position: Midfielder
Birth date: June 17, 1990
Birth place: Sunderland
Height: 1.82m (6ft)
Clubs: Sunderland, Coventry (loan), Liverpool
International: England

HENDERSON ON...

CLUB AND COUNTRY

"It's a bit different playing for club and country. Just the way that we play the game for England you get more time on the ball. The style of play is different. When you play in the Premier League against the top teams you spend most of the time chasing the ball. You have to take your chances when you get them."

SCORING

"I don't score many goals but it is something I enjoy so I am working on that and hopefully I will get more in the future. It is vital to get goals from midfield and that's what I need to do."

HIS APPROACH

"I want to become a much better player, improve every day, keep working hard and learn from the players around me. I'm very appreciative of where I am today but I still want more. I want to strive for more and keep that hunger going. I am not really fussed about where I play, I just want to play football but obviously I like to play in the middle."

WHAT HIS TEAM MATE SAYS...

"When someone tells him he can't do something or that he's not good enough, it's straight on to the training ground to prove them wrong. He just wants to improve and is a nice, grounded young lad.".

Darren Bent, *England striker and former Sunderland colleague.*

5 HENDERSON FACTS

1. The midfielder was days off his 21st birthday when he moved from Sunderland to Liverpool in June 2011, for a fee that could hit £20m.

2. Henderson was Sunderland's Young Player of the Year for 2010 and 2011.

3. He's played for England at Under-19, 20, 21 and senior levels.

4. You are more likely to find him putting in extra training than going out to nightclubs.

5. He took on England Under-21 colleague Alex Oxlade-Chamberlain at a game of keepy-uppy with a tennis ball and won with 148 to 136.

EXTRA TIME Henderson was bought by former boss Kenny Dalglish with the aim of the player becoming the new Steven Gerrard. The current Reds captain has actually hailed his fellow midfielder as his potential successor at Anfield.

FRAIZER CAMPBELL

Sunderland and England striker

FACT FILE

FRAIZER CAMPBELL

Position: Striker
Birth date: September 13, 1987
Birth place: Huddersfield
Height: 1.7m (5ft 8in)
Clubs: Manchester United, Royal Antwerp (loan), Hull City (loan), Tottenham (loan), Sunderland
International: England

CAMPBELL ON...

BEING A FAN

"When I was a youngster I didn't support a team, just Andy Cole! I model myself on him because I watched him such a lot. He still gives me tips on how to improve my game."

JOINING THE FANS

"When I was out injured I went to lots of grounds and joined the fans in the stands. I tried to go in disguise but it didn't last long. I didn't mind because the supporters were amazing."

ENGLAND DEBUT

"It was fantastic to play for my country and I'll work hard to get another chance. From when you're 10-years-old, that's what you think about, playing for your favourite club or playing for your country."

LEAVING MAN UNITED

"I always believed I had made the right decision. At the time I left they had loads of strikers there, world-class strikers too. I could see I was not going to get much of an opportunity. I needed to go. I still think it was a great decision."

WHAT HIS BOSS SAYS...

"His attitude has just been fantastic, he's so, so positive. He's just magnificent to have around the place."
Martin O'Neill, *Sunderland manager*

CAMPBELL FACTS

2. After 18 months out with injury, Campbell returned to action in January 2011 and scored a goal in each of his first two games.

3. One of his big pals is Man City's Joleon Lescott – who he loves to beat on video games such as Call of Duty.

4. Former Sunderland boss, and ex-Man United player Steve Bruce, signed Campbell from the Old Trafford side for £3.5m in 2009.

1. His partner Emma gave birth to their daughter as he took to the pitch for his England debut!

5. He scored four goals and won 14 caps at England Under-21 level.

EXTRA TIME Campbell played 32 Championship games whilst on loan at Hull City in 2007-08. He hit 15 league goals and helped the Tigers to the play-off final where they beat Bristol City to reach the Premier League for the first time ever.

SHOOT ANNUAL 2013 **33**

THE DIFFICULT GAME!

HOW DO YOU THINK YOU ARE DOING SO FAR? NO CHEATING WE HOPE — ALTHOUGH YOU MIGHT GET SOME HELP FROM FRIENDS AND FAMILY!

41. Name of Wolverhampton Wanderers ground?

A: ....

42. Manager who guided Reading to promotion in 2012.

A: ....

....

43. How tall, in metres, is striker Peter Crouch?

A: ....

44. The second part of Plymouth football club's full name.

A: ....

45. Which Premier League side are known as the Citizens?

A: ....

46. City in which Russian side Zenit play.

A: ....

47. Which striker was named 2012 PFA Player of the Year?

A: ....

48. The three teams relegated from the Championship at the end of 2011-12.

A: ....

....

....

49. Which two clubs went out of the Football League in 2012?

A: ....

....

50. Who was England manager before Fabio Capello?

A: ....

....

51. Last pair of brothers to appear together in the same England team.

A: ....

....

52. In which country do Porto play?

A: ....

53. From which club did Everton buy forward Tim Cahill?

A: ....

54. How much did Chelsea pay to buy striker Fernando Torres?

A: ....

55. In which year did Steven Gerrard make his Liverpool debut: 1996, 1998, 2000?

A: ....

56. Which London team won League One in 2011-12?

A: ....

....

57. Former Man United legend who is now an actor and film star.

A: ....

....

58. Name of Blackpool's home ground.

A: ....

59. Matt Le Tissier scored 47 from 48 penalty-kicks for Southampton. True or false?

A: ....

WOW!

60. Club whose nickname in the Glovers.

A: ....

TOP TEN LISTS

Goals, points, money - these are the best in the Premier League and the world!

WORLD'S MOST VALUABLE CLUBS

1. Man United — £1.17b
2. Real Madrid — £916m
3. Arsenal — £753m
4. Bayern Munich — £662m
5. Barcelona — £616m
6. AC Milan — £529m
7. Chelsea — £415m
8. Juventus — £397m
9. Liverpool — £349m
10. Inter Milan — £279m

EUROPEAN LEAGUES' TOP SCORERS 2011-12

1. Lionel Messi (Barcelona) — 50
2. Cristiano Ronaldo (Real Madrid) — 45
3. Bas Dost (Heerenveen) — 32
4. Burak Yilmaz (Trabzonspor) — 32
5. Robin van Persie (Arsenal) — 30
6. Klass Jan Huntelaar (Schalke) — 29
7. Zlatan Ibrahimovic (AC Milan) — 28
8. Wayne Rooney (Man United) — 27
9. Wesley (Vaslui) — 27
10. Mario Gomez (Bayern Munich) — 26

FOOTBALL'S HIGHEST EARNERS

1. Lionel Messi (Barcelona) — £27.4m
2. David Beckham (LA Galaxy) — £26.15m
3. Cristiano Ronaldo (Real Madrid) — £24.3m
4. Samuel Eto'o (Anzhi) — £19.3m
5. Wayne Rooney (Man United) — £17.09m
6. Sergio Aguero (Man City) — £15.6m
7. Yaya Toure (Man City) — £14.6m
8. Fernando Torres (Chelsea) — £13.86m
9. Kaka (Real Madrid) — £12.86m
10. Philipp Lahm (Bayern Munich) — £11.87m

BARCLAYS PREMIER LEAGUE

MOST POINTS

1. Man United — 1,663
2. Arsenal — 1,449
3. Chelsea — 1,402
4. Liverpool — 1,334
5. Aston Villa — 1,089
6. Tottenham — 1,086
7. Everton — 1,034
8. Newcastle — 1,017
9. Blackburn — 969
10. Man City — 784

MOST LEAGUE APPEARANCES

1. Ryan Giggs — 573
2. David James — 573
3. Gary Speed — 535
4. Sol Campbell — 503
5. Frank Lampard — 491
6. Emile Heskey — 488
7. Paul Scholes — 465
8. Jamie Carragher — 463
9. Phil Neville — 460
10. Alan Shearer — 441

MOST GOALS

1. Alan Shearer — 260
2. Andy Cole — 189
3. Thierry Henry — 176
4. Robbie Fowler — 163
5. Michael Owen — 149
6. Les Ferdinand — 149
7. Frank Lampard — 148
8. Teddy Sheringham — 147
9. Wayne Rooney — 137
10. JF Hasselbaink — 127

EXTRA TIME Three players hit double-figures in the race to be top scorer in the 2011-12 Champions League. Barcelona's Lionel Messi had 14; Bayern Munich's Mario Gomez got 12 and Cristiano Ronaldo of Real Madrid 10.

DOUBLING UP

Do you remember which of these players played for the same team? We want you to match them up in pairs to the team they have both played turned out for. It might not have been at the same time and it may even have been on loan! We've helped you by including badges of the teams.

GAEL CLICHY

BRAD FRIEDEL

MICHAEL CARRICK

GARETH BARRY

DARREN BENT

ASHLEY COLE

SHAY GIVEN

SEB LARSSON

Arsenal

AVFC
PREPARED

BLACKBURN ROVERS F.C.
18 75
ARTE ET LABORE

BIRMINGHAM CITY
FOOTBALL CLUB
· 1875 ·

ANSWER 1

PLAYERS NAME

PLAYERS NAME

CLUB

ANSWER 2

PLAYERS NAME

PLAYERS NAME

CLUB

ANSWER 3

PLAYERS NAME

PLAYERS NAME

CLUB

ANSWER 4

PLAYERS NAME

PLAYERS NAME

CLUB

EXTRA TIME Keeper John Burridge turned out for 29 clubs between 1969 and 1997. He played 771 League games in England and Scotland, and at 43 years and 162 days was the oldest player to appear in the Premier League.

SHOOT ANNUAL 2013   37

WHICH BALL?

THE PREMIER LEAGUE BALL FLIES SO FAST THAT SOMETIMES THE KEEPER DOESN'T KNOW WHERE IT WILL END UP NEXT! THAT'S WHY SHOT-STOPPERS CAN'T AFFORD ONE SECOND OF RELAXATION. NOW YOU HAVE TO BE JUST AS SMART AS THE BEST KEEPERS AROUND BY DECIDING WHICH OF THE BALLS ARE THE REAL ONES FROM THESE TOP-FLIGHT MATCHES. WRITE YOUR ANSWERS IN THE SPACES PROVIDED AND THEN YOU CAN CHECK YOUR ANSWERS ON PAGE 78.

GAME ONE

GAME TWO

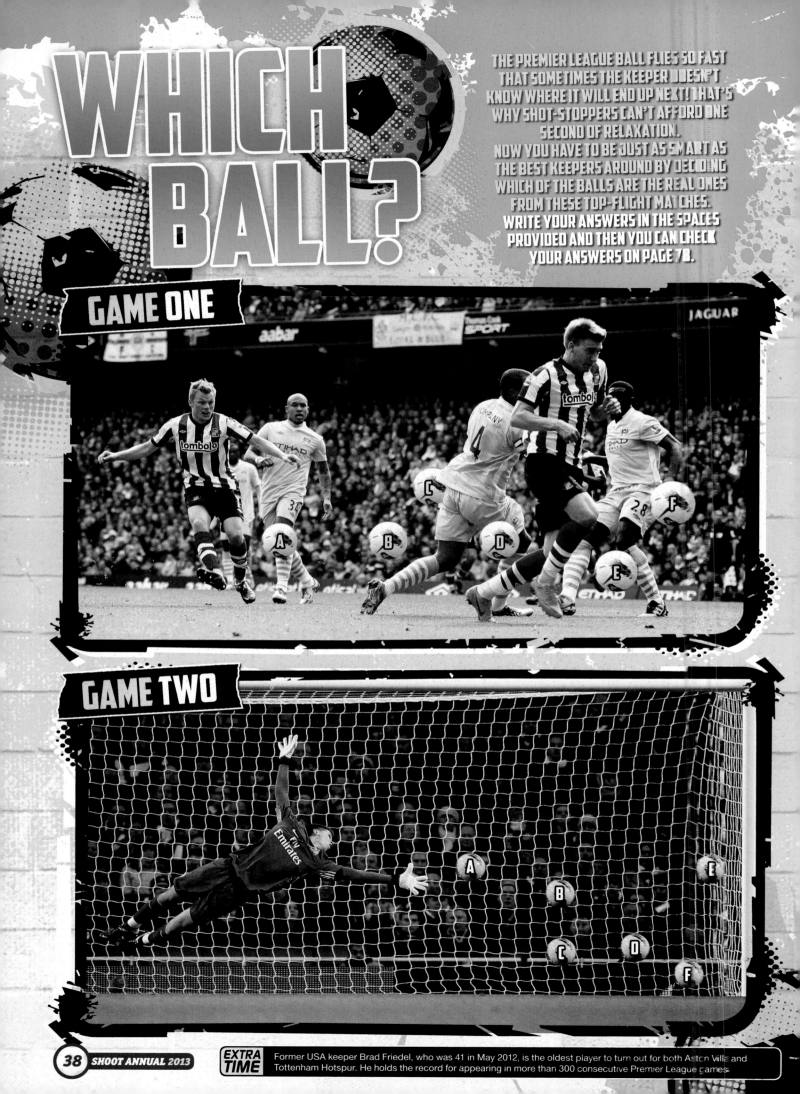

EXTRA TIME Former USA keeper Brad Friedel, who was 41 in May 2012, is the oldest player to turn out for both Aston Villa and Tottenham Hotspur. He holds the record for appearing in more than 300 consecutive Premier League games

GAME THREE

GAME FOUR

GAME ONE: MAN CITY v SUNDERLAND

The correct ball is:

GAME TWO: ARSENAL v EVERTON

The correct ball is:

GAME THREE: ASTON VILLA v CHELSEA

The correct ball is:

GAME FOUR: MAN UNITED v CHELSEA

The correct ball is:

MICHAEL DAWSON
Tottenham and England defender

FACT FILE

MICHAEL RICHARD DAWSON

Position: Defender
Birth date: November 18, 1983
Birth place: Northallerton, North Yorkshire
Height: 1.9m (6ft 3in)
Clubs: Nottingham Forest, Tottenham
International: England

DAWSON ON...

CRITICISM

"When I get criticism it hurts, believe me, no matter how thick skinned you are. Maybe some is deserved and maybe some is not but it is how you deal with it and bounce back. I'm always critical of myself. I have high standards. I am a footballer and I want to play. You work as hard as you can in training to make sure you are in on Saturday."

ENGLAND

"It was a special moment to walk out in an England shirt and a great honour to play for your country. To start the match was fantastic. The Premier League, the national team, the Champions League are all important. For me, playing in the Champions League can only help my England chances."

HARRY REDKNAPP

"He's a big believer in his players. Even when I wasn't playing I knew he still had a lot of belief in me."

5 DAWSON FACTS

1. He was in England's provisional squad for the 2010 World Cup finals but missed the cut.

2. Dawson's older brothers, Andy and Kevin, have both played League football.

3. He joined Tottenham from Forest a fee of £4m in January 2005 and is now contracted to 2015..

4. When he was a teenager he used to help the local milkman with deliveries.

5. He made his England Under-21 debut the same day as striker Darren Bent.

WHAT HIS FORMER BOSS SAYS...

"His contribution in the dressing room is excellent and he is fearless on the pitch. He wants to defend for his life. What a competitor!"
Harry Redknapp, Ex-*Spurs* manager

EXTRA TIME Tottenham captain Dawson suffered a further blow to his international ambitions when he suffered an ankle injury in March 2012 which dashed all hope he had of making England's 23-man squad for Euro 2012.

VINCENT KOMPANY
Manchester City and Belgium defender

FACT FILE
VINCENT KOMPANY
Position: Defender
Birth date: April 10, 1986
Birth place: Uccle, Belgium
Height: 1.93m (6ft 4in)
Clubs: Anderlecht, Hamburg, Manchester City
International: Belgium

KOMPANY ON...

MANCHESTER
"I feel comfortable and I am ready to stay here a long time. We have a strong group and my challenge is to go into the dressing room and keep up the momentum there and not just on the pitch."

MONEY
"If a good player comes in I don't care what he is on. He could be on Queen's wages. I am happy, I was brought up like that. If I have a big cheque or a small cheque I will always play for the same reason. You have a short career and must make the most of it."

WINNING THE TITLE
"Lots of people want me to talk about moving, but what interests me is Manchester City. We can't stop with the title. We want to win the Champions League."

WHAT HIS BOSS SAYS...

"He is a strong defender, who has improved a lot in the last two or three years. He is a leader and our captain, one of the best defenders in Europe now and someone who can still improve a lot."
Roberto Mancini,
Manchester City manager

5 KOMPANY FACTS

1. Kompany was named Barclays Premier League Player of the Season for leading City to the 2011-12 title.

2. His Belgium team mate Eden Hazard was France's Player of the Season fellow Belgian Jan Vertonghen won the award in Holland.

3. He is a FIFA ambassador for SOS Children's Villages and works with disadvantaged children in the Congo, the country where his father was born.

4. Kompany forked out £6,000 to buy a guitar at a charity auction organised by former team mate Shay Given.

5. He lists Belgian waffles and a drop of red wine as two of his favourite items.

EXTRA TIME: only did Kompany become the first Manchester City captain to lift England's title for the first time in 44 years – also headed the only goal as his side beat rivals United 1-0 in the vital game at the Etihad Stadium in April 2012.

SHOOT ANNUAL 2013 **41**

HAIR RAISING

We all know players make some weird and wonderful style statements. But last season hair became the major talking point with some amazing barnets! There were some crazy days in the past but bad hair days now appear the norm...

Here are some of the wackiest with our marks out of ten (ten being bad!)

FABRICIO COLOCCINI
NEWCASTLE

MARGUANE FELLAINI
EVERTON

DAVID LUIZ
CHELSEA

These guys must have the same style gurus! The puffed out curly locks on these three certainly standout! They could almost be compared to Valderrama... check on the panel on the right!

BAD HAIR DAY: 7

PAUL SCHARNER
AUSTRIA

ALEX SONG
ARSENAL

NEYMAR
SANTOS

Song has progressed as a player and what more can state this than his... hair? The colour and style change almost by the week. So there is no telling what it looks like when you read this...

This guy's hair goes in keeping with his Brazilian roots. The wonder boy could set some new standards when he finally arrives in European football.

The vibrant colours of Scharner's hair don't match his image as a hard-hitting midfielder! He's stood out since arriving in the Premier League – his performances haven't been bad either!

BAD HAIR DAY: 8

BAD HAIR DAY: 6
(He is Brazilian!)

BAD HAIR DAY: 8

EXTRA TIME Wayne Rooney, who is thought to have paid £30,000 for his hair transplant in 2011, admitted: "I was going bald at 25, why not. I'm delighted with the result." Clinics reported a 65 per cent rise in work after Rooney's operation.

BENOIT ASSOU-EKOTTO
TOTTENHAM

Err, we can't really explain this one! Don't be surprised to see something totally different when he takes to the pitch.

BAD HAIR DAY: 9

BACARY SAGNA
ARSENAL

Can you figure out the thinking behind the haircut of Sagna? No? Neither can we! The hair MUST go! Please email us if you know what is going on with his locks.

BAD HAIR DAY: 10

MARIO BALOTELLI
MAN CITY

CHEICK TIOTE
NEWCASTLE

They could have Mohicans... or something that looks like a giant truck tyre ran over their heads. In Mario's case you expect madness. Tiote... well he's hard, so we think it looks great pal!

BAD HAIR DAY: 7

HAIR OF THE SEASON

WAYNE ROONEY
MAN UNITED

Of course this award has to go to Manchester United and England forward Wayne Rooney for this transformation. Were the new locks worth the cash? Well he appears to have got value for money.

BEFORE

GOOD HAIR DAY: 10

AFTER

EXTRA TIME Carlos Valderrama was Colombia's keeper from 1985 to 1998 when he earned a record 111 caps for his country – and scored 11 international goals! He was also a bit handy at free-kicks and laying on goals for team-mates!

SHOOT ANNUAL 2013 **43**

WHO DID THEY PLAY FOR?

ALAN SHEARER
MATCH OF THE DAY

GARY LINEKER
MATCH OF THE DAY

CHARLIE NICHOLAS
SKY SPORTS

PHIL THOMPSON
SKY SPORTS

JEFF STELLING
SKY SPORTS

ANDY TOWNSEND
ITV

GARETH SOUTHGATE
ITV

Many top **TV** pundits and presenters used to play football for some very famous clubs. But can you match up the star names to the badges of the sides where they were as famous on the pitch as they are now off it?
Oh…one of the guys never played football professionally so we've put his favourite team's badge on the page instead…

FCB

Arsenal

BARCELONA

ARSENAL

YOU'LL NEVER WALK ALONE
LIVERPOOL
FOOTBALL CLUB
EST. 1892

MIDDLESBROUGH
FOOTBALL CLUB
1876

AVFC
PREPARED

LIVERPOOL

MIDDLESBROUGH

ASTON VILLA

HARTLEPOOL UNITED F.C.
1908

NEWCASTLE UNITED

HARTLEPOOL UNITED

NEWCASTLE UNITED

SPOT THE PLAYER

Some players have surnames you simply can't forget. We want you to match the first names of the players to the picture that gives us their second name.

JAMES _____

STEPHEN _____

DAMIEN _____

STEPHEN _____

JOE _____

JOE _____

ALEX OXLADE-CHAMBERLAIN

Arsenal and England midfielder

FACT FILE

ALEXANDER MARK DAVID OXLADE-CHAMBERLAIN

Position: Winger
Birth date: August 15, 1993
Birth place: Portsmouth
Height: 1.8m (5ft 1in)
Clubs: Southampton, Arsenal
International: England

CHAMBERLAIN ON...

WALCOTT COMPARISONS

"People will compare me with Theo as we came here at a similar age and from the same club. But we are different players. Theo is a winger or striker whilst I have always been an attacking midfielder who has gone out wide. He is a great player. I have belief in myself and in my ability."

HIS MANAGER

"I trust the boss to progress me as he is a top man, very intelligent. The young boys get lots of chances here in the cups and it is a great place to learn."

ARSENAL

"It's been a tough challenge but I knew when I signed that I would have to work hard. There are quality players at this club and a quality manager. I know that I have to keep working hard and learn off the boys and hopefully the rest will come."

THIERRY HENRY

"Thierry was my hero. He used to try stuff and pull it off, fantastic stuff. I remember that goal he scored against Tottenham in 2002, ran through the whole team. When he came back to Arsenal, I was a bit shy and nervous for the first two weeks. He was sat two spots away, with Theo Walcott in the middle. It was surreal."

5 CHAMBERLAIN FACTS

1. Chamberlain had made just 43 appearances for Southampton when Arsenal bought him for £12m in summer 2011.

2. Manchester City were also interested in Chamberlain, but he fancied working alongside boss Arsene Wenger.

3. His father Mark made his England debut at 21. Alex was 18 when he pulled on a senior shirt for the first time!

4. Chamberlain made his Southampton debut at the age of 16 years and 199 days – but Theo Walcott is still the Saints' youngester-ever player!

5. He was named in the PFA League One Team of the Year in 2010-11 as Southampton gained promotion.

WHAT HIS BOSS SAYS...

"He is a fighter, with personality. In a short period of time he has become an important player who can make a difference. He has improved quickly."

Arsene Wenger, *Arsenal manager*

EXTRA TIME Despite his father and uncle both playing professional football, Chamberlain almost went into rugby! His school played the oval ball game and cricket and he was offered a trial at London Irish. Southampton blocked the move.

FACT FILE
SEAMUS JOHN JAMES GIVEN

Position: Keeper
Birth date: April 20, 1976
Birth place: Lifford, Ireland
Height: 1.85m (6ft 1in)
Clubs: Blackburn, Swindon (loan), Sunderland (loan), Newcastle, Manchester City, Aston Villa
International: Republic of Ireland

GIVEN ON...

LEAVING ST. JAMES' PARK

"At one point I did think I would be at Newcastle for life but things change and you change yourself. Sometimes you can go a bit stale at one club but when I left it felt right. It gave me a new lease of life. I enjoyed my time there but in the last few months I thought I needed to try something new."

LEAVING MANCHESTER CITY

"I didn't even start a pre-season friendly, so I think I could read into that. But Joe Hart had a great season so you have to take in on the chin. We spent a lot of time together and tried to help each other. I've no issues with Joe or anyone at City. Joe is going to be one of the very best around for many years."

JOINING VILLA

"I want to repay Villa for giving me a chance. The Villa staff and fans have been fantastic towards me and I am really enjoying my football again. I hope to be playing beyond 40. I came here to prove I am still a top Premier League keeper."

INTERNATIONAL DEBUT

"I was 19 at the time, so it's a good few years ago and a few wrinkles ago, but it was a momentous occasion for me and my family. I was very proud to play for my country."

WHAT HIS TEAM MATE SAYS...

"A hero to young keepers I meet because of the way he has worked and applied himself and the standards he has set. He is anxious when he can't train or play. He always wants to be 100 per cent fit."
Kevin Kilbane, *Republic of Ireland*

5 GIVEN FACTS

1. Given joined Newcastle United in 1997 and was sold to Manchester City in January 2009 for £7m.

2. Aston Villa paid Manchester City £3.5m to buy Given in summer 2011.

3. He played 462 games for Newcastle United putting him second in the club's all-time appearance records.

4. Shay and his wife Jayne organise many events to raise cash for the fight against cancer, having lost his mother to the disease when he was a child.

5. Given has twice been named Ireland's Player of the Year, in 2005 and 2006.

EXTRA TIME Shay Given made his Republic debut against Russia in March 1996 and with more than 120 international games to his name is Ireland's most-capped player. He and winger Kevin Kilbane reached 100 caps in the same match.

SHOOT ANNUAL 2013 47

KIDS' STUFF

Ever wondered when some of the Premier League's top players started to make the grade in football?

We can reveal some of them were still at school when it all started happening for them… Even at a very young age some current and recent England internationals were looking good for a career in the professional game when they turned out for the country's schoolboys. The English Schools FA run tournaments on a regular basis all around the country to find the best teams and best players who go on to represent the Three Lions. Here are a few of the many who have made their names in the top-flight after starting at that level.

Michael Owen, *1995*

England's second-highest scorer ever was on the goal trail even as a 15-year-old schoolboy international and hit 12 goals in eight games in 1995. Owen became a full international at the age of 18 and his career has taken in Liverpool, Real Madrid, Newcastle and Manchester United.

Phil Neville, *1992*

The Everton captain and former Man United midfielder and defender progressed from school boys to full international level where his versatility made him a vital asset for a number of managers. Expected to go into coaching and management when he retires.

Wes Brown, *1995*

The central defender joined Sunderland from Manchester United in summer 2011 after more than 360 games for the Old Trafford side. Was once described by former boss Sir Alex Ferguson as one of the club's best natural defenders.

Scott Parker, *1996*

Parker has only recently established himself as a full senior international, but has captained his country. Yet he's been turning out for his country since he was at school! The 2011 Footballer of the Year also played for England at Under-16, 18 and 21 levels.

EXTRA TIME England's most-capped player is Peter Shilton (1970-90) with 125 international appearances. David Beckham (1996-) has 115 caps, Bobby Moore (1962-73) 108, Bobby Charlton (1958-70) 106 and Billy Wright (1946-59) 105.

Joe Cole, 1997

Cole had a great 2011-12 on loan from Liverpool to French side Lille. He has also played for West Ham and Chelsea. A naturally gifted midfielder who many fans feel should have been given a lot more England chances.

Jermain Defoe, 1997

One of the best natural finishers around, Defoe's career has taken in West Ham, Portsmouth, a loan at Bournemouth and then Tottenham. It's amazing to think that none of his appearances for England until the end of 2011-12 have been for the full 90 minutes – yet he still has an international hat-trick to his name!

Chris Smalling, 2008

The defender was signed to Maidstone United when he starred for England schoolboys against Scotland at Wembley. Fulham liked what they saw and signed him. He then moved to Man United in a £10m deal. At 21 he made his full England debut – just three years after playing at Under-18 schools level!

Nicky Butt, 1990

The battling midfielder, best remembered for his time at Man United and Newcastle, has been rated by Sir Alex Ferguson as one of the best youngsters he has brought through the ranks.

Danny Murphy, 1992

After starting his career at Crewe, the midfielder went on to play for Liverpool, Charlton, Tottenham and then Fulham were he became captain and a vital part of their squad.

Leon Osman, 1997

Despite being hit by a serious injury earlier in his career, the midfielder has played more than 300 games for Everton, where he made his top-flight debut in 2004-05.

and finally.... Ryan Giggs, 1989

Giggsy in an England shirt? Oh yes, it did happen, despite the fact he was born in Cardiff! He was eligible to play because of where he lived, in Manchester, and captained the side. He later played 64 times for Wales and scored 12 goals.

See the stars of tomorrow!

For more details of England Schoolboys and their forthcoming fixtures visit www.esfa.co.uk

WHICH CLUBS WHERE THEY AT?

WE KNOW YOU ARE SMART ENOUGH TO RECOGNISE WHO THESE PLAYERS ARE AND EVEN WHICH CLUBS' SHIRTS THEY ARE PICTURED IN. BUT WE WANT YOU TO MATCH THEM UP WITH THE KIT FROM THEIR PREVIOUS TEAMS. **WRITE THE NAMES OF THE TWO CLUBS IN THE ANSWERS PANEL, ALONG WITH THE CORRECT LETTER FOR THEIR FORMER SIDE'S SHIRT**

A

B

C

D

E

F

PETER CROUCH
CURRENT CLUB
PREVIOUS CLUB (LETTER)

CESC FABREGAS
CURRENT CLUB
PREVIOUS CLUB (LETTER)

SCOTT PARKER
CURRENT CLUB
PREVIOUS CLUB (LETTER)

DANIEL STURRIDGE
CURRENT CLUB
PREVIOUS CLUB (LETTER)

LUIS SUAREZ
CURRENT CLUB
PREVIOUS CLUB (LETTER)

DAVID DE GEA
CURRENT CLUB
PREVIOUS CLUB (LETTER)

EXTRA TIME Scott Parker began his career at Charlton in 1997 before moving to Chelsea for £10m in 2004. They sold him to Newcastle for £6.5m in 2005. West Ham bought him in 2007 for £7m. Spurs paid £5.5m for him in summer 2011.

YOUR GUIDE TO THE CLUBS

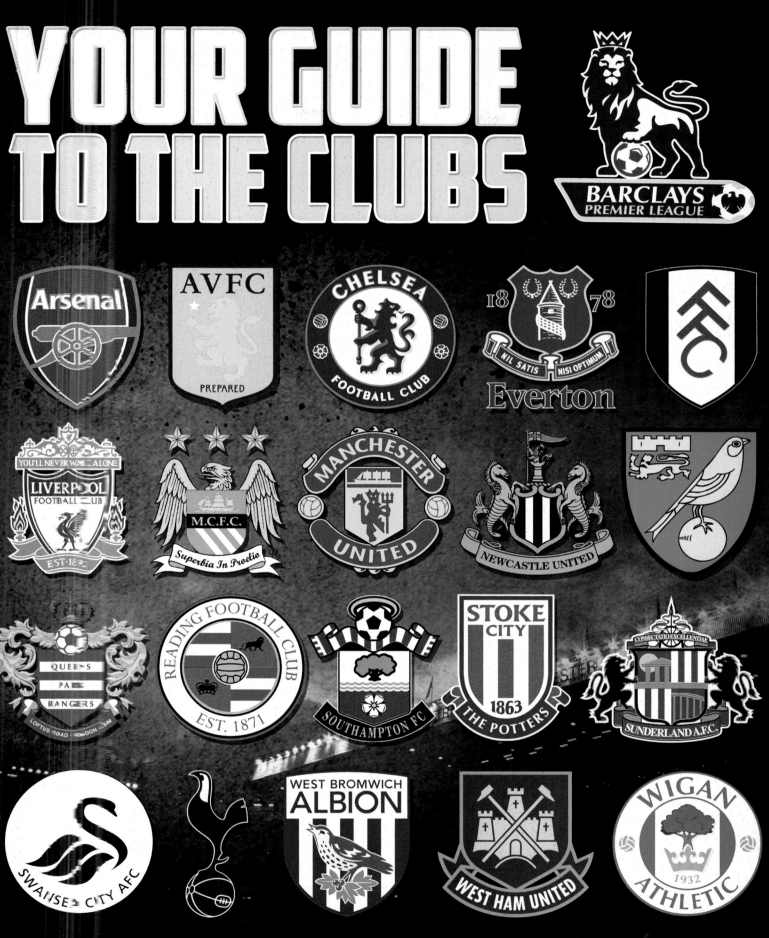

BARCLAYS PREMIER LEAGUE

FACTS ABOUT ALL 20 ENGLISH PREMIER LEAGUE SIDES
PLUS STAR PLAYERS, SCORERS, STATS AND DETAILS FROM SEASON 2011-12

ARSENAL

TOP SCORER: Robin van Persie, 37
PLAYER OF THE SEASON:
Robin van Persie
BEST CROWD: 60,111 v Chelsea
BEST RESULT: Arsenal 5 Spurs 2
MEMORABLE MOMENT: It could have been beating AC Milan 3-0 in the Champions League at the Emirates. But the 5-2 home win over Spurs after being 2-0 down takes some beating...

ASTON VILLA

TOP SCORER: Darren Bent, 10
FANS' PLAYER OF THE SEASON:
Stephen Ireland
BEST CROWD: 40,053 v Chelsea
BEST RESULT: Chelsea 1 Aston Villa 3
MEMORABLE MOMENT: It was a pretty forgettable season for Villa fans, but when captain Stiliyan Petrov was diagnosed with leukemia the fans came out in numbers to support him in the home defeat to Chelsea.

CHELSEA

TOP SCORER: Frank Lampard, 16
PLAYER OF THE SEASON:
Juan Mata
BEST CROWD: 41,830 v Tottenham
BEST RESULT: B. Munich 3 Chelsea 4
MEMORABLE MOMENT: The Blues finished a disappointing sixth, but Roberto Di Matteo took them to FA Cup victory and then the penalty shoot-out success against Bayern in the European Cup Final.

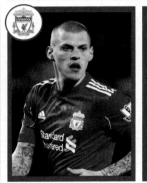

EVERTON

TOP SCORER: Nikica Jelavic, 11
PLAYER OF THE SEASON:
John Heitinga
BEST CROWD: 39,517 v Newcastle
BEST RESULT: Everton 1 Man City 0
MEMORABLE MOMENT: Everton famously came from 4-2 down to draw at Old Trafford – a result that eventually cost United the title. The Toffees finished seventh, four points ahead of Mersey rivals Liverpool.

FULHAM

TOP SCORER: Clint Dempsey, 23
PLAYER OF THE SEASON:
Clint Dempsey
BEST CROWD: 25,700 v Arsenal
BEST RESULT: Fulham 6 QPR 0
MEMORABLE MOMENT: Fulham had another decent season, finishing ninth. The Cottagers defeated Arsenal, Liverpool and Newcastle but the sweetest moment was thrashing rivals QPR 6-0 at the Cottage.

LIVERPOOL

TOP SCORER: Luis Suarez, 17
PLAYER OF THE SEASON:
Martin Skrtel
BEST CROWD: 45,071 v Man United
BEST RESULT: Liverpool 3 Cardiff 2
MEMORABLE MOMENT: The Reds had a dismal League campaign, finishing eighth. But they reached the FA Cup Final and won the League Cup after a penalty shoot-out against Cardiff City.

MANCHESTER CITY

TOP SCORER: Sergio Aguero, 30
PLAYER OF THE SEASON:
Sergio Aguero
BEST CROWD: 48,000 v QPR
BEST RESULT: Man City 3 QPR 2
MEMORABLE MOMENT: Two late, late goals snatched their first-ever Premier League title away from their fiercest rivals. Mancini's men also beat the Red Devils twice, including 6-1 at Old Trafford!

MANCHESTER UNITED

TOP SCORER: Wayne Rooney, 35
FANS' PLAYER OF THE SEASON:
Antonio Valencia
BEST CROWD: 75,627 v Wolves
BEST RESULT: Man United 8 Arsenal 2
MEMORABLE MOMENT: The Red Devils steamrollered the Gunners to win 8-2, but despite some great performances Sir Alex Ferguson's troops had to settle for a first season in six without silverware.

NEWCASTLE UNITED

TOP SCORER: Demba Ba, 16
PLAYER OF THE SEASON:
Fabricio Coloccini
BEST CROWD: 52,389 v Man City
BEST RESULT: Newcastle 3 Man United 0
MEMORABLE MOMENT: The Magpies had a terrific season under Alan Pardew. Demba Ba and Papiss Cisse went goal crazy in a year the Toon beat Sunderland, Chelsea, Man United and Liverpool.

NORWICH CITY

TOP SCORER: Grant Holt, 17
PLAYER OF THE SEASON:
Grant Holt
BEST CROWD: 26,819 v Liverpool
BEST RESULT: Tottenham 1 Norwich 2
MEMORABLE MOMENT: The Canaries enjoyed a fantastic first season back in the Premier League, comfortably finishing 12th. The high was beating Champions League hopefuls Spurs at White Hart Lane.

QUEENS PARK RANGERS

TOP SCORER: Heidar Helguson, 9
FANS' PLAYER OF THE SEASON:
Clint Hill
BEST CROWD: 18,076 v Man City
BEST RESULT: QPR 1 v Chelsea 0
MEMORABLE MOMENT: On top of beating their Champions League-winning neighbours, the R's beat Liverpool, Arsenal, Swansea, Tottenham and Stoke in their final five home games.

READING

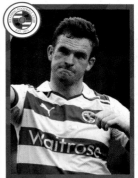

TOP SCORER: Adam Le Fondre, 12
PLAYER OF THE SEASON:
Alex Pearce
BEST CROWD: 24,026 v West Ham
BEST RESULT: Reading 3 Southampton 1
MEMORABLE MOMENT: Brian McDermott led the Royals back to the Premier League after a 1-0 win at home to Nottingham Forest. They returned to the top-flight for a second time after a four-year break.

SOUTHAMPTON

TOP SCORER: Rickie Lambert, 31
FANS' PLAYER OF THE SEASON:
Rickie Lambert
BEST CROWD: 32,363 v Coventry
BEST RESULT: Saints 1 West Ham 0
MEMORABLE MOMENT: Saints secured back-to-back promotions on the final day against Coventry. Nigel Adkins side won 4-0 to return to the Premier League after a seven-year absence.

STOKE CITY

TOP SCORER: Peter Crouch, 14
PLAYER OF THE SEASON:
Peter Crouch
BEST CROWD: 27,739 v Aston Villa
BEST RESULT: Stoke 1 Liverpool 0
MEMORABLE MOMENT: The Potters went on a Europa League adventure and after surviving two qualifying rounds and the group stage drew Valencia. Stoke lost 1-0 in both legs.

SUNDERLAND

TOP SCORER: Stephane Sessegnon
Nicklas Bendtner, Sebastian Larsson, 8
PLAYER OF THE SEASON:
Stephane Sessegnon
BEST CROWD: 47,751 v Newcastle
BEST RESULT: Sunderland 1 Man City 0
MEMORABLE MOMENT: The Black Cats replaced boss Steve Bruce with Martin O' Neill who won ten of his first 15 games, including the victory over Man City.

SWANSEA CITY

TOP SCORER: Danny Graham, 14
PLAYER OF THE SEASON:
Michel Vorm
BEST CROWD: 20,605 v Liverpool
BEST RESULT: Swansea 1 Man City 0
MEMORABLE MOMENT: The Swans passed their first-ever Premier League test with top marks after great victories against Manchester City, Arsenal and Liverpool along the way.

TOTTENHAM HOTSPUR

TOP SCORER: Emmanuel Adebayor, 18
FANS' PLAYER OF THE SEASON:
Scott Parker
BEST CROWD: 36,274 v Arsenal
BEST RESULT: Tottenham 2 Arsenal 1
MEMORABLE MOMENT: Spurs started the season on fire and looked like title challengers. The turning point came with the 3-2 defeat at Manchester City. Their form then slipped and they finished fourth.

WEST BROMWICH ALBION

TOP SCORER: Peter Odemwingie, 11
PLAYER OF THE SEASON:
Jonas Olsson
BEST CROWD: 26,358 v Arsenal
BEST RESULT: Villa 1 West Brom 2
MEMORABLE MOMENT: West Brom finally established themselves as a Premier League side after comfortably surviving a second-consecutive season. Wins at Liverpool and Villa were the highlights.

WEST HAM UNITED

TOP SCORER: Carlton Cole, 15
PLAYER OF THE SEASON:
Mark Noble
BEST CROWD: 35,000 v Hull City
BEST RESULT: West Ham 2 Blackpool 1
MEMORABLE MOMENT: The Hammers beat Cardiff in the Championship play-off semis before a Ricardo Vaz Te winner saw off Blackpool 2-1 in the final. West Ham returned to the Premier League in a year.

WIGAN ATHLETIC

TOP SCORER: Franco di Santo, 7
PLAYER OF THE SEASON:
Gary Caldwell
BEST CROWD: 22,187 v Newcastle
BEST RESULT: Wigan 1 Man United 0
MEMORABLE MOMENT: The Latics were doomed heading into the final two months of the season, but victories at Liverpool and Arsenal plus home wins over Man United and Newcastle United ensured safety.

TOP FLIGHT
STATS, FACTS & TRIVIA YOU NEED TO KNOW!

PREMIER LEAGUE 2011-12

Manchester City's title-winning stars are believed to have pocketed a bonus of £250,000 each for lifting the Premier League trophy. For most of them that's less than two weeks' wages!

Senegal striker Papiss Cisse, who joined Newcastle in January 2012, equalled the Premier League record of 13 goals in his first 12 games.

HIGHEST TOTAL HOME ATTENDANCES

Man United	1,432,358
Arsenal	1,140,006
Newcastle	948,777
Man City	893,851
Liverpool	840,808
Chelsea	788,089
Sunderland	742,813
Tottenham	684,501
Aston Villa	643,590
Everton	631,333
Stoke	517,290
Norwich	505,509
Wolves	487,967
Fulham	480,576
West Brom	471,165
Bolton	449,729
Blackburn	428,474
Swansea	378,978
Wigan	354,038
QPR	328,613

The 1,066 goals scored during the campaign was a new Premier League record and included 19 hat-tricks.

Aston Villa's seven victories all season was their worst in 120 years.

Wayne Rooney's goal for Man United at Sunderland on the final day took his club career tally to 199.

Eight times during David Moyes's ten years at Goodison Park Everton have finished in the top seven.

Jermain Defoe's strikes last term meant he became the first Premier League player to score 20 goals playing as a sub.

EXTRA TIME Hot-shot Senegal striker Papiss Cisse became the first Newcastle United player to win Premier League goal of the season for the second of his stunning strikes when the Magpies won 2-0 at Chelsea late in the campaign

Arsenal have qualified for the Champions League every full season that Arsene Wenger has been their manager.

When Man City won the title on the final day against QPR they faced a player who turned out in almost 100 games for them – Nedum Onuoha.

Spurs scored in every home league game of the season for the first time in 40 years.

BAD GUYS

Most disciplinary points:
Joey Barton (QPR) 14

Most reds:
Joey Barton (QPR) 2
Mario Balotelli (Man City) 2
Djibril Cisse (QPR) 2
David Wheater (Bolton) 2

Norwich City's return to the top-flight after a six-year absence saw them finish 12th and earn more than £7m in prize money.

Franco Di Santo's goal for Wigan when they beat Wolves 3-2 on the final day of the season was the Latics' 2,000th in League football.

Some 100 penalties were awarded during the season but 28 of them were missed!

England's top league had only finished level on points and had to be decided on goal difference or average on five previous occasions.

The average age of a Premier League player in 2011-12 was 26.35 years. Norwich City had the youngest average at 25.08 and Stoke City the oldest at 28.42.

TOP SCORERS

Robin van Persie (Arsenal) 30
Wayne Rooney (Man United) 27
Sergio Aguero (Man City) 23
Clint Dempsey (Fulham) 17
Yakubu (Blackburn) 17
Emmanuel Adebayor (Spurs) 17

MOST ASSISTS

David Silva (Man City) 15
Antonio Valencia (Man United) 13
Juan Mata (Chelsea) 13
Emmanuel Adebayor (Spurs) 11
Alex Song (Arsenal) 11

Man City's season got off to a poor start when they were beaten 3-2 by neighbours United in the Community Shield.

Man City's Joe Hart won the Golden Glove for most Premier League clean sheets for a second successive year. The England keeper recorded 17 games without conceding – one worse than the previous campaign. He was two clean sheets ahead of Holland and Newcastle shot-stopper Tim Kurl (Newcastle) 15

EXTRA TIME Top-flight new boys Swansea City not only wowed fans with their great passing game – they also won the Fair Play Award after finishing the 2011-12 Premier League with the best behaved players!

SHOOT ANNUAL 2013 55

UNBELIEVABLE!

CITY'S AMAZING LAST-DAY TITLE-CLINCHER

The last time Manchester City won the English title current boss Roberto Mancini was just three-years-old!

Forty-four years of hurt ended for the blue half of Manchester in the most dramatic of styles when their Italian manager clinched the Premier League crown in the dying seconds of the 2011-12 season.

And it was almost a carbon copy of their previous title win in 1967-68.

All those years ago City won the title on the final day when they beat Newcastle 4-3 and Man United were runners-up.

In 2012 they had to beat QPR on the final day – and once again it was their neighbours United who finished second.

But few fans could have imagined just how dramatic the final stages of the campaign would turn out to be.

Both Manchester sides went into the final day level on points but City top on superior goal difference.

When United took the lead at Sunderland through Wayne Rooney after 20 minutes it meant they went top of the table. But when Pablo Zabaleta put City ahead against QPR on 39 minutes it meant the blue half of Manchester were back on top.

Djibril Cisse's equaliser for Rangers just after half time meant it was then advantage United. And it got even better for the Red Devils when Jamie Mackie put QPR 2-1 ahead.

With City into injury time at the Etihad Stadium it looked like United had both hands back on the Premier League trophy. But then Edin Dzeko levelled the scores. United started to sweat. But surely City couldn't score twice in the time added on and with just seconds left on the clock?

The game at Sunderland had finished when the unbelievable happened – Segio Aguero hit a winner and the title was City's on goal difference.

Two teams from the same City but only one winner!

THEIR TITLE-WINNING STARS

TOP SCORER: Sergio Aguero 23
MOST ASSISTS: David Silva 15
BAD BOY: Mario Balotelli, 2 red cards

WHAT THE BOSS SAID...

"We have beaten United two times, we have scored more than them and conceded less so we deserve it. I never gave up. It was a crazy finish to the game and the season but the best team won the title. We now need to improve and I am very happy because for an Italian to win the title here in England is fantastic for all Italian people." **Roberto Mancini,** *Man City manager*

WHAT THE PLAYERS SAID...

This season has been unbelievable, so emotional, there are no words to describe how it happened. For all the club legends and fans who have waited so long, I'm so, so happy."
Vincent Kompany, *City captain*

"We have fantastic players, they are growing. They have fantastic talent and next year we will get more cups."
Yaya Toure, *Ivory Coast midfielder*

"I am really happy. The truth is we can hardly believe it ourselves. We thought the Premier League had gone. We got two goals in five minutes, it was absolutely unbelievable." **Sergio Aguero,** *match-winning striker*

FINAL TABLE 2011-12

	Team	PL	GD	PTS
01	Man City	38	64	89
02	Man United	38	56	89
03	Arsenal	38	25	70
04	Tottenham	38	25	69
05	Newcastle	38	5	65
06	Chelsea	38	19	64
07	Everton	38	10	56
08	Liverpool	38	7	52
09	Fulham	38	-3	52
10	West Brom	38	-7	47
11	Swansea	38	-7	47
12	Norwich	38	-14	47
13	Sunderland	38	-1	45
14	Stoke	38	-17	45
15	Wigan	38	-20	43
16	Aston Villa	38	-16	38
17	QPR	38	-23	37
18	Bolton	38	-31	36
19	Blackburn	38	-30	31
20	Wolves	38	-42	25

FINAL TABLE 1967-68

	Team	PL	GD	PTS
01	Man City	42	42	58
02	Man United	42	34	56
03	Liverpool	42	31	55
04	Leeds	42	30	53
05	Everton	42	27	52
06	Chelsea	42	-6	48
07	Tottenham	42	11	47
08	West Brom	42	13	46
09	Arsenal	42	4	44
10	Newcastle	42	-1	41
11	Nt'm Forest	42	-12	41
12	West Ham	42	4	38
13	Leicester	42	-5	38
14	Burnley	42	-7	38
15	Sunderland	42	-10	37
16	Southampton	42	-10	37
17	Wolves	42	-9	36
18	Stoke	42	-23	35
19	Sheff Wed	42	-12	34
20	Coventry	42	-20	33
21	Sheff United	42	-21	32
22	Fulham	42	-42	27

CHAMPIONSHIP
ROYAL RULERS

Reading started the season slowly then mounted a sprint finish to catapult themselves back into the Premier League after a four-year absence.

Manager Brian McDermott suffered heartbreak when his Royals were beaten in the 2011 play-off final – but bounced back in style by lifting the Championship title.

Amazingly his side were in 16th spot in November but then won 15 of their final 17 games.

Southampton gained their second successive promotion having also finished as runners-up in League One the previous campaign. The Saints returned to the Premier League after seven years out of the top-flight and after surviving a financial scare that could have seen them go out of business.

At the other end of the table, Coventry City were relegated to the third tier of English football for the first time in 48 years and financially troubled Portsmouth were demoted to the third tier after 30 years away. Doncaster Rovers dropped down a division after four years in the Championship.

CHAMPIONSHIP
PLAY-OFF FINAL

West Ham bounced back to the Premier League at the first attempt despite Blackpool's brave battling at Wembley.

Striker Carlton Cole put the Hammers ahead after 35 minutes but Blackpool refused to give up and equalised through Tom Ince on 48.

With the game looking set to go into extra-time Ricardo Vaz Te hit a winner on 87 minutes.

Hammers boss Sam Allardyce admitted: "It was a very difficult game for us, especially after they equalised. The result was all that really mattered, though, and we couldn't have scored the winner at a better time.

Blackpool manager Ian Holloway added: "I'm just sorry the lads didn't get the bonus they deserved, but we can still feel proud. Half the world thought West Ham were going to win but it didn't feel that way halfway through the second half."

CHAMPIONSHIP FINAL TABLE

		PL	GD	PTS
01	Reading	46	28	89
02	Southampton	46	33	88
03	West Ham	46	33	86
04	Birmingham City	46	27	76
05	Blackpool	46	20	75
06	Cardiff City	46	13	75
07	Middlesbrough	46	1	70
08	Hull City	46	3	68
09	Leicester	46	11	66
10	Brighton	46	0	66
11	Watford	46	-8	64
12	Derby	46	-8	64
13	Burnley	46	3	62
14	Leeds United	46	-3	61
15	Ipswich Town	46	-8	61
16	Millwall	46	-2	57
17	Crystal Palace	46	-5	56
18	Peterborough	46	-10	50
19	Nott'm Forest	46	-15	50
20	Bristol City	46	-24	49
21	Barnsley	46	-25	48
22	Portsmouth	46	-9	40
23	Coventry City	46	-24	40
24	Doncaster Rovers	46	-37	36

WEST HAM UNITED

2011-12 STATS

TOP SCORERS
Ricky Lambert (*Southampton*) 25
Ricardo Vaz Te (*West Ham*) 21*
Billy Sharp (*Southampton*) 19**
Ross McCormack (*Leeds*) 18
Marlon King (*Birmingham*) 16
Kevin Phillips (*Blackpool*) 16
Matt Fryatt (*Hull*) 16
Charlie Austin (*Burnley*) 16
*10 for Barnsley, **10 for Doncaster

MOST ASSISTS
Chris Burke (*Birmingham City*) 16

BAD BOYS
Most disciplinary points:
Barry Robson (*Middlesbrough*) 14
Most reds: Neil Danns (*Leicester City*); Habib Beye (*Doncaster*); Matt Mills (*Leicester*) 2

HIGHEST AVERAGE ATTENDANCE: West Ham 31,079

LEAGUE ONE
VALLEY HIGH

CHARLTON ATHLETIC

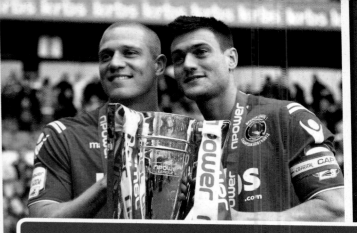

Former Charlton defender Chris Powell guided Athletic to the League One title in his first full year in charge.

The fans' favourite, who earned five England caps during his playing days at the Valley, turned around the fortunes of a side that were struggling when he took over in January 2011.

Relegated from the Premier League in 2007 they fell into League One in 2009. They were last season's league leaders from September onwards.

Wednesday won the battle of the Sheffield sides for automatic promotion, pipping neighbours United to second on the final day.

Founder members of the Premier League, they were relegated in 2000 and two years later were in the third-flight. They returned to the Championship in 2005 but dropped into League One in 2010.

Wycombe and Chesterfield were relegated back to League Two after just one season, Rochdale after two years and Exeter after three at this level.

LEAGUE ONE FINAL TABLE

		PL	GD	PTS
01	Charlton Athletic	46	46	101
02	Sheffield Wednesday	46	33	93
03	Sheffield United	46	41	90
04	Huddersfield	46	32	81
05	MK Dons	46	37	80
06	Stevenage	46	25	73
07	Notts County	46	12	73
08	Carlisle	46	-1	69
09	Brentford	46	11	67
10	Colchester	45	-5	59
11	Bournemouth	46	-4	58
12	Tranmere	46	-4	56
13	Hartlepool	46	-5	56
14	Bury	46	-19	56
15	Preston North End	46	-14	54
16	Oldham	46	-16	54
17	Yeovil	46	-21	54
18	Scunthorpe	46	-4	52
19	Walsall	46	-6	50
20	Leyton Orient	46	-27	50
21	Wycombe Wanderers	46	-23	43
22	Chesterfield	46	-25	42
23	Exeter City	46	-29	42
24	Rochdale	46	-34	38

2011-12 STATS

TOP SCORERS
Jordan Rhodes *(Huddersfield)* **35**
Ched Evans *(Sheffield United)* **28**
Bradley Wright-Phillips *(Charlton)* **20**
Gary Madine *(Sheffield Wed)* **18**

MOST ASSISTS
Clayton Donaldson *(Brentford)*
Stephen Quinn *(Sheffield United)* **13**

BAD BOYS
Most disciplinary points:
Stephen Gleeson *(MK Dons)* **14**
Most reds: Neil Bishop *(Notts County)*;
Andy Butler *(Walsall)* **2**

HIGHEST AVERAGE ATTENDANCE
Sheffield Wednesday 21,336

LEAGUE ONE
PLAY-OFF FINAL

Huddersfield beat Yorkshire rivals Sheffield United in a dramatic shoot-out at Wembley. After extra-time the two sides were still goal less and following an astonishing 21 penalties, Blades keeper Steve Simonsen missed his spot-kick to hand victory to the Terriers. Town keeper Alex Smithies had already scored to make it 8-7.

EXTRA TIME The Football League play-offs were first introduced at the end of season 1986-87. The Conference, England's fifth tier and first non-League competition, adopted the same format in 2002-03 and lower divisions have followed suit.

LEAGUE TWO
TALK OF THE TOWNS

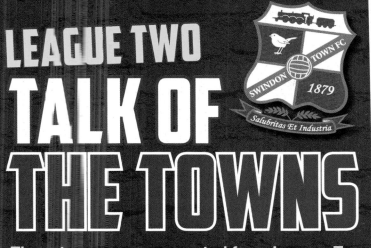

Three towns were promoted from League Two – including Swindon, champions at the first attempt under debut boss Paolo Di Canio.

The Italian, a former hero at West Ham, took over the Robins shortly after they were relegated the previous season. Despite the heartbreak of losing both his parents during the course of the campaign, the new manager kept his promise of taking the side back up a division.

Shrewsbury, managed by Graham Turner, won promotion with a game to spare, helped by their unbeaten home record. The previous season he had guided the Shrews to fourth on his return to the club he had last bossed in 1984.

Crawley's third-place finish saw them promoted for the second successive season. They won the 2011 Conference after spending big on players and earned their League One spot with a win on the final day of the season at Accrington.

Hereford United were relegated back to the Conference after a six-year stay in League football that saw them rise to League One for two years.

Macclesfield Town also returned to the Conference after 15 years in League football.

2011-12 STATS

TOP SCORERS
Jack Midson (AFC Wimbledon),
Izale McLeod (Barnet),
Adebayo Akinfenwa (Northampton)
Lewis Grabban (Rotherham) 18
Marc Richards (Port Vale) 16

MOST ASSISTS
Ryan Hall (Southend United) 19

BAD BOYS
Most disciplinary points:
Joseph Martin and Charlie Lee
(both Gillingham) 14

HIGHEST AVERAGE ATTENDANCE
Bradford City 10,171

LEAGUE TWO FINAL TABLE

		PL	GD	PTS
01	Swindon Town	46	43	93
02	Shrewsbury Town	46	25	88
03	Crawley Town	46	22	84
04	Southend United	46	29	83
05	Torquay United	46	13	81
06	Cheltenham Town	46	16	77
07	Crewe Alexandra	46	8	72
08	Gillingham	46	17	70
09	Oxford United	46	11	68
10	Rotherham United	46	4	67
11	Aldershot	46	2	66
12	Port Vale	46	8	59
13	Bristol Rovers	46	-10	57
14	Accrington Stanley	46	-12	57
15	Morecambe	46	6	56
16	AFC Wimbledon	46	-16	54
17	Burton Albion	46	-27	54
18	Bradford City	46	-5	50
19	Dagenham and Redbridge	46	-22	50
20	Northampton Town	46	-23	48
21	Plymouth Argyle	46	-17	46
22	Barnet	46	-27	46
23	Hereford United	46	-20	44
24	Macclesfield Town	46	-25	37

LEAGUE TWO
PLAY-OFF FINAL

Nick Powell and Byron Moore scored as Crewe Alexandra beat Cheltenham 2-0 to return to League One after three seasons.

Powell's wonder goal came after a quarter of an hour and Moore's with eight minutes to go.

Cheltenham had won both their previous play-off appearances in 2002 and 2006.

EXTRA TIME Crewe were unbeaten in their previous 18 games before the play-off final at Wembley against Cheltenham Town. The match was watched by a crowd of 24,000. The Robins had dominated the game but still lost.

ALL THE WINNERS!

WHO WON WHAT IN 2011-12

CHAMPIONS LEAGUE

CHELSEA

Didier Drogba signalled the end of his eight-year spell with Chelsea by firing the Blues to European Cup glory. His side fell behind to a Thomas Muller goal for Bayern Munich after 83 minutes but the Ivory Coast striker headed a brilliant equaliser after 89. After extra-time Drogba hit the 4-3 penalty shoot-out winner with the last kick of the game at the Allianz Arena.

CHAMPIONSHIP CHAMPIONS

READING

AUTOMATIC PROMOTION	PLAY-OFF FINAL
SOUTHAMPTON	BLACKPOOL 1 WEST HAM 2

RELEGATED
COVENTRY CITY, PORTSMOUTH, DONCASTER

EXTRA TIME Chelsea's 2012 Champions League victory made them only the sixth British side to win the European Cup after Liverpool (5 times), Manchester United (3), Nottingham Forest (2), Celtic and Aston Villa (both 1).

LEAGUE ONE CHAMPIONS
CHARLTON

AUTOMATIC PROMOTION	PLAY-OFF FINAL
SHEFF WEDNESDAY	SHEFFIELD UNITED 0 HUDDERSFIELD 0
	HUDDERSFIELD 8-7 ON PENS

RELEGATED
WYCOMBE WANDERERS, CHESTERFIELD, EXETER CITY, ROCHDALE

LEAGUE TWO CHAMPIONS
SWINDON TOWN

AUTOMATIC PROMOTION	PLAY-OFF FINAL
SHREWSBURY TOWN CRAWLEY TOWN	CHELTENHAM 0 CREWE 2

RELEGATED
HEREFORD, MACCLESFIELD TOWN

CONFERENCE
FLEETWOOD

PLAY-OFF FINAL
LUTON 1 YORK CITY 2

SCOTTISH PREMIER LEAGUE
CELTIC

Neil Lennon (left) managed the Bhoys to their 43rd title, 20 points ahead of Rangers who had ten points deducted.

SCOTTISH CUP
HEARTS

Hearts beat Edinburgh rival Hibs 5-1 with goals from Darren Barr, Rudi Skacel (two), Danny Grainger (pen) and Ryan McGowan. James McPake replied.

SCOTTISH LEAGUE CUP
KILMARNOCK

A goal from substitute Dieter van Tournhout just 11 minutes after he took to the pitch gave Killie a 1-0 victory over Celtic in front on 49,572 fans.

EXTRA TIME Striker Richie Allen picked up TWO title medals in 2012. He was in the Fleetwood squad that won promotion to the Football League as Conference champions – and was on loan at Fylde who won the Evo-Stick First Division North.

LEAGUE CUP

LIVERPOOL

Joe Mason gave Cardiff the lead after 19 minutes and Martin Skertel equalised on the hour for Liverpool to take the game to extra-time. Dirk Kuyt put the Reds ahead only for Ben Turner to force the game to penalties. Liverpool won 3-2.

JOHNSTONE'S PAINTS TROPHY

CHESTERFIELD

An own goal by Swindon Town defender Oliver Risser gave Chesterfield the lead on 46 minutes and Craig Westcarr made it 2-0 in time added on

FA CUP

CHELSEA

Didier Drogba made it four finals, four goals, four wins as the Blues lifted the trophy. Ramires gave Chelsea the lead on 11 minutes, Drogba made it 2-0 on 52 and Andy Carroll got a consolation for the Reds on 64.

EXTRA TIME Didier Drogba scored 157 goals in 341 games for Chelsea after joining them from Marseille in July 2004 for a then club record £24m. He lifted three Premier League titles, four FA Cups, two League Cups and the European Cup.

PFA YOUNG PLAYER OF THE YEAR

KYLE WALKER

The 22-year-old Tottenham full back had a season to remember. Not only did he win this award but he also made his full England debut and became a father for the first time. Walker joined Spurs from Sheffield United in 2009.

PFA PLAYER OF THE YEAR AND FOOTBALL WRITERS' FOOTBALLER OF THE YEAR

ROBIN VAN PERSIE

After his Arsenal side made one of their worst-ever starts to a season Dutchman van Persie rescued them almost single-handed. He scored a total of 37 goals in 47 appearances for the Gunners in 2011-12, which included 30 Premier League goals in 38 matches. That took him to 132 goals for the club.

FA TROPHY FINAL

NEWPORT COUNTY 0
YORK CITY 2

York were back in the final three years after they failed to win the trophy. This time there was no mistake with goals from Matty Blair and Lanre Oyebanjo.

FA VASE FINAL

DUNSTON UTS 2
WEST AUCKLAND TOWN 0

Andrew Bulford scored both goals for the Gateshead side – making him the first player to score in every round of the competition last term, even in replays!

EUROPA LEAGUE FINAL

ATLETICO MADRID 3
ATHLETIC BILBAO 0

Colombian striker Radamel Falco scored twice in the first half and Diego in the last five minutes as the Spanish side won in front of a 52,300 crowd in Bucharest.

SPAIN LA LIGA	ITALY SERIE A	FRANCE LIGUE 1	GERMANY BUNDESLIGA	HOLLAND EREDIVISIE
CHAMPIONS REAL MADRID	CHAMPIONS JUVENTUS	CHAMPIONS MONTPELLIER	CHAMPIONS BORUSSIA DORTMUND	CHAMPIONS AJAX
RUNNER-UP BARCELONA	RUNNER-UP AC MILAN	RUNNER-UP PARIS SG	RUNNER-UP BAYERN MUNICH	RUNNER-UP FEYENOORD

EXTRA TIME Real Madrid's La Liga victory in 2011-12 gave them a Spanish record of 32 titles. Their 100 points, 121 goals, 16 away victories and plus-89 goal difference were also new bests. They were nine points clear of rivals Barcelona.

FUNNY OLD GAME

SHOOT TAKES A LIGHTER LOOK AT FOOTBALL

PUTTING THE BOOT ON...

The choice was amazing and England striker Daniel Sturridge wishes his mum had gone with him to help select a new pair of boots!

WE ARE FLYING...

Ben Foster's invisible jet pack made him very difficult to follow.

NET EFFECT

The opposition decided that the only way to stop Papiss Cisse was to trap him like a fish in a net. It still didn't work...

SHINE ON...

Ooops... do you reckon someone forgot to take their boots to the game?

BOG OFF!

Bolton keeper Adam Bogdan tried his best but he still couldn't touch his nose with his tongue.

WHO WAS IT?

Supporters were convinced that someone in the stands had eaten beans for their lunch.

GOOD TACKLE!

Luis Suarez's decision to try out rugby worked a treat on Eveton's John Heitinga.

TALL TALE

Mario Balotelli needed to check out if the tail was real… after all, most of his life is totally unreal!

BUM DEAL

Now you know why Tomas Rosicky likes playing for Arsenal…

GO ON PUSH…

Ref Mike Jones wasn't impressed when Fernando Torres missed another chance and dished out 20 press-ups.

ROCKY ON!

The press and fans were stunned by Paolo Di Canio's surprise recruit for Swindon Town. All he would admit to was being called Rocky…

IN SYNCH... NOT!

West Brom's Gareth McAuley and QPR's Jamie Mackie failed badly when they tried synchronised dancing at the Hawthorns.

NO SNORE DRAW...

The game against Everton proved a touch too boring for Sunderland boss Martin O'Neill and his club's fans…

CHILD'S PLAY

The clubs reckoned their youth policies were really paying off.

SPOT THE DIFFERENCE!

CHELSEA V MAN UNITED

A

B

EXTRA TIME There were TEN goals in the two Premier League games involving Chelsea and Man United in 2011-12. United won 3-1 at Old Trafford and the sides drew 3-3 at Stamford Bridge – the Red Devils coming back from 3-0 down!

HERE ARE PICTURES FROM TWO BIG GAMES — AND WE'VE LET OUR DESIGNER MAKE SIX CHANGES TO EACH PHOTOGRAPH. ALL YOU HAVE TO DO IS BE MORE EAGLE-EYED THAN THE BEST PREMIER LEAGUE REFEREE AND SEE IF YOU CAN SPOT THE DIFFERENCES! PICTURE A IS THE ORIGINAL SO DRAW RINGS AROUND THE DIFFERENCES IN PICTURE B.

NEWCASTLE V MAN CITY

A

B

EXTRA TIME Manchester City completed a Premier League double over Newcastle United in 2011-12 as they won their first top tier title for 44 years. City won 3-1 at home and 2-0 at St. James' Park in the last but one game of the season.

SHOOT ANNUAL 2013 **71**

TOP TRIVIA

THE GOOD, THE BAD AND THE RIDICULOUS FROM THE SOMETIMES WEIRD WORLD OF FOOTBALL!

EGGSCELLENT!

Chickens were on the transfer wish list of a Premier League club to save a bit of cash and give their players the freshest eggs. Fulham stars munch their way through dozens of eggs after training, so director Karim Al Fayed suggested a small holding where they could rear chickens and get fresh eggs.

YOU HUMM IT...

Fancy being able to play like Wayne Rooney? What you need is a CD by The Hummingbirds... The England and Manchester United striker reckons their tunes help him to play better and he has to listen to them before every game. Bet it won't last when he discovers that most of the group support Liverpool!

JUST SWEETIES...

Aaron Lennon and Shaun Wright-Phillips have been outed as being sweet-toothed! Their England team mate Jermain Defoe has spilled the beans on the pair by revealing that winger Lennon just loves Haribo: "He opens a packet every time we get on the team bus." And fellow wide man SWP is a devil for doughnuts according the to striker: "He gets loads of Krispy Kreme doughnuts sent from Harrods."

CHOP, CHOP!

Manchester United and England defender Chris Smalling is better known to his team-mates as Hong Kong, after animated television superhero Hong Kong Phooey! As a youngster Smalling was a bit useful at judo!

LIONEL WHO?

Forget Lionel Messi's record five goals in a Champions League game – Ray Crawford did it years ago! The former Ipswich Town striker hit five against Floriana in 1963 when the competition was known as the European Cup – and got a £10 bonus for each strike!

HOME GAME

No need to worry about rain or mud if you are a mate of Phil Neville – you can play football inside his house! And there's no danger of getting into trouble for smashing up the place either as the Everton captain has built an indoor pitch!

The former England midfielder's five-a-side set up comes complete with goals and grass painted on the floor. Wife Julie said: "Like we don't have enough football, now we have a pitch inside our house."

ROCKING!

Tomas Rosicky is set to deafen his Arsenal team-mates. They were already aware that the Czech Republic star quite fancied himself as a rocker after teaming up with a band from his home country. But now the midfielder is learning how to play heavy metal riffs on an electric guitar. And the bad news for his fellow Gunners is that Rosicky looks up to Metallica axeman Kirk Hammett. It's not the R and B stuff they are used to at the Emirates Stadium…

WHO ARE YA?

Out of this world – Dr Who could have been a professional footballer! Actor Matt Smith, who plays the Tardis-travelling Time Lord played in the youth sides of Northampton, Nottingham Forest and Leicester City. After suffering a serious back injury he turned to acting instead. Ood* about that then?

Ood are aliens in the BBC series!

WOULD YOU BELIEVE IT?

Joey Howe kissed his girlfriend after scoring a hat-trick for his side in Sussex – and was sent-off for leaving the pitch!

In 2012, former England captain David Beckham became the first man to grace the cover of women's magazine Elle.

A linesman who punched a player for disputing a decision was sent off by a referee in Hampshire.

Plucky Nova think they set a new record when they were beaten 58-0 by Wheel Power in a Torbay Sunday League game in 2012. They were just 20-0 down at half time!

Jack Swan went on a tour of Stoke City's training ground – and was called onto the pitch by boss Tony Pulis to join in a kickabout

The crowd was sent home at half time when the referee at a Ryman Division One South game in Surrey was stung by a bee!

WAYNE'S WORLD

PLANET FOOTBALL ACCORDING TO THE MANCHESTER UNITED AND ENGLAND STRIKER

PLAYING POSITION

"I don't care where I play. I am just happy to be on the pitch. Maybe not right back, but midfield is a role where you can get on the ball and influence the game a bit more. I don't care if I don't score so long as we win."

AMBITION

"I'm a player who wants to do well all of the time and know I can improve. I keep working and practising but I don't really set myself targets, although an injury free season would be nice. I hope I am going to get better."

LIONEL MESSI

"Messi is a great player and rightly won World Player of the Year. Barca have their style of play and not everyone can play like they do. Their biggest asset is that when they lose the ball they all defend and try to win it back again."

MAN UNITED

"It's always disappointing when you lose. To play for Manchester United you have a big responsibility. You always feel responsible whether you are 20 or 35. I am more experienced although I can only help the young ones so much as they have great ability."

EXTRA TIME Rooney won his 50th cap for England in 2009 when he was just 23. It came in a 2-1 World Cup 2010 qualifier victory against Ukraine at Wembley. Former Three Lions captain David Beckham had won 19 caps at the same age.

PLAYING LIVERPOOL

"It's the toughest place to go and win a game. All my family are Everton fans and to beat Liverpool is a great feeling and a great day. It's a big day for United but for me it's a massive game."

LEADERSHIP

"I've captained England and United on one-off occasions but to get the jobs full-time would be a great honour."

TRAINING

"I am the type of person if I do no training I could put on a lot of weight, so I watch what I eat."

HAIR TRANSPLANT

"I was going bald and found it stressful. I thought 'why not' and I spend more time looking in the mirror now."

STAYING AT MANCHESTER UNITED

"It's the best decision I've made in my football career. The manager has put his faith in a lot of younger players and everyone should be excited by them."

FACT FILE

WAYNE MARK ROONEY

Position: Striker
Birth date: October 24, 1985
Birth place: Liverpool
Height: 1.76m (5ft 9in)
Clubs: Everton, Manchester United
International: England

WHAT HIS BOSS SAYS...

"Wayne is ready now to take his career up a further notch and become a leader himself. He has shown tremendous improvement in his temperament and his reactions to tackles and things over the past few years. As maturity comes along it brings other things. It brings responsibility. He is improving all the time."

Sir Alex Ferguson,
Manchester United manager

ROONEY'S MEMORABLE DATES

October 24, 1985: *Born in Croxteth, Liverpool*
August 17, 2002: *Made his Everton debut*
October 2, 2002: *First senior goal*
February 12, 2003: *Became England's youngest-ever player*
August 31, 2004: *Joined Man United for £30m*
September 28, 2004: *United debut and hat-trick v Fenerbahce*
June 15, 2006: *World Cup finals debut v Trinidad and Tobago*
July 1, 2006: *Sent-off in World Cup game v Portugal*
March 30, 2009: *England Player of the Year 2008*
March 1, 2010: *England Player of the Year 2009*
April 24, 2010: *PFA Player of the Year*
April 22, 2012: *Named in PFA Premier League Team of the Year.*

EXTRA TIME Rooney was England's youngest-ever player on his debut against Australia in 2003. That best was beaten by Theo Walcott in 2006. Wayne is still the country's youngest scorer, netting against Macedonia in September 2003.

SHOOT ANNUAL 2013 **75**

ALL THE ANSWERS

PAGE 10-11 FAMOUS FACES

1982 Alex McLeish and
      Sir Alex Ferguson
1985 Brian McDermott
1987 Sir Alex Ferguson
1989 Ryan Giggs
1990 Alan Shearer
1992 Alan Pardew
2000 Steven Gerrard

PAGE 12-13 QUIZ PART 1

01. Berbatov (5)
02. False
03. Bayern Munich
04. Blackburn Rovers
05. Chilean
06. Defender/right back
07. Twente
08. Belgium
09. Ivory Coast
10. Brentford
11. Dutch
12. Nemanja Vidic
13. Wigan
14. Wales
15. Papiss Cisse
16. Manchester United
17. Petr Cech
18. Pep Guardiola
19. Moritz Volz
20. Russia

PAGE 14-15 SPOT THE BOSS

PAGE 22-23 QUIZ PART 2

21. 4
22. Camp Nou
23. Arsenal
24. Ryan Giggs
25. Ajax
26. Euros and World Cup
27. Sir Alex Ferguson

28. 18
29. Lewis Hamilton
30. San Siro
31. 10
32. Hearts
33. Brazil
34. Thierry Henry
35. LA Galaxy
36. Swansea City
37. 90,000
38. Emirates Stadium
39. Monaco
40. Robbie Keane

PAGE 28 NAME THAT PLAYER

A. Wayne Rooney
B. Frank Lampard
C. James Milner
D. Jack Wilshere

PAGE 29 CHAMP CHALLENGE

A. Birmingham City, Blues
B. Ipswich, Tractor Boys
C. Millwall, Lions
D. Blackpool, Tangerines
E. Brighton, Seagulls
F. Crystal Palace, Eagles

PAGE 34-35 QUIZ PART 3

41. Molineux
42. Brian McDermott
43. 2
44. Argyle
45. Man City
46. St. Petersburg
47. Robin van Persie
48. Doncaster Rovers,
    Portsmouth, Coventry City
49. Hereford, Macclesfield Town
50. Steve McClaren
51. Gary and Phil Neville
52. Portugal
53. Millwall
54. £50m
55. 1998
56. Charlton Athletic
57. Eric Cantona
58. Bloomfield Road
59. True
60. Yeovil Town

PAGE 38-39 WHICH BALL

Game 1: D   Game 2: F
Game 3: B   Game 4: B

PAGE 44 WHO DID THEY PLAY FOR?

Gary Lineker, Barcelona
Alan Shearer, Newcastle
Charlie Nicholas, Arsenal
Phil Thompson, Liverpool
Gareth Southgate &
Andy Townsend, both played for
Aston Villa and Middlesbrough
Jeff Stelling, Hartlepool fan!

PAGE 45 SPOT THE PLAYER

James **PERCH**
Damien **DUFF**
Joe **COLE** (coal)
Stephen **CARR**
Stephen **IRELAND**
Joe **HART** (heart)

PAGE 50 WHICH CLUBS

Peter Crouch,
Stoke City, B Tottenham
Cesc Fabregas,
Barcelona, E Arsenal
Scott Parker,
Tottenham, F West Ham
Daniel Sturridge,
Chelsea, C Man City
Luis Suarez, Liverpool, D Ajax
David de Gea,
Man United, A Atletico Madrid

PAGE 70-71 SPOT THE DIFFERENCE

VAN'S THE MAN!

Arsenal and Holland striker Robin Van Persie will never forget season 2011-12.

He was the Gunners' Player of the Season, PFA Players' Player of the Year, Football Writers' Footballer of the Year and also fired 37 goals to pick up the Golden Boot.

RVP also got a special trophy from sponsors Barclays for hitting 30 Premier League goals.

VISIT WWW.SHOOT.CO.UK
The amazing football website!

All the latest football news, interviews, blogs and more.

OVER 600,000 HITS A MONTH!

Scan with your mobile device to learn more.

SHOOT HANBOOK
The ultimate football guide!
OUT NOW

Handbook of Football 2013

A-Z OF TEAMS
RECORD BREAKERS
TOP SCORERS
SUPER SIDES
EURO CHAMPS
WORLD CHAMPS
SUPERSTARS
BEST PLAYER STATS

Cover is subject to change and approval.

DOWNLOAD TODAY

The fantastic Shoot app!

Now you can download the magazine to all popular mobile devices, iPads and computers.

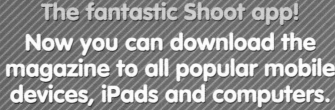

Available on the App Store

Available on Android

Scan with your mobile device to learn more.